A Geomantic Guidebook to

Touchstones for Today

Designing for Earth harmony with stone arrangements

by Alanna Moore

Python Press
Australia

Alanna Moore is the author of:
Backyard Poultry – Naturally, 1998.
Stone Age Farming - 2001, 2nd edition 2013.
Divining Earth Spirit - 1994, 2nd edition 2004.
The Magic of Menhirs & Circles of Stone - 2005.
The Wisdom of Water - 2007.
Sensitive Permaculture - 2009.
Water Spirits of the World - 2008, 2nd edition 2012.

Touchstones for Today - previously published as The Magic of Menhirs & Circles of Stone and now updated and greatly expanded in this 2013 edition.

ISBN – 978-0-9757782-5-8

Published by **Python Press**
www.pythonpress.com
pythonpress@gmail.com
PO Box 929 Castlemaine Vic
3450 Australia

Text, design, graphics and photos by Alanna Moore,
except for photos on pages 3, 28, 113, 118 and the back cover - by Peter Cowman.

Proudly produced in central Victoria, Australia.
Printed on acid free paper by Lightning Source Inc., a company committed to manufacturing books in a manner that both respects the environment and helps preserve the world's natural resources.

With thanks for help given by:
Peter Cowman, British Society of Dowsers, Stockholm Society of Dowsers, Tom Graves, Billy Gawn, David Cowan, Wojcech Pukarski, David Lockwood, Junitta Vallak.

Copyright © Alanna Moore 2013

All rights reserved. No reproduction, copy or transmission of this publication may be made without written permission of the publisher, in accordance with the provisions of the Copyright Act.

Front cover: A Stone Altar in Co. Roscommon, Ireland
- well maintained amidst the ruins of an old church.
Next page: The author at a 'check-in' point, ahead of
a Stone Circle in Co. Kerry, Ireland.

Touchstones for Today

by Alanna Moore

Contents

Introduction   7

Chapter 1: Ancient Traditions   9

Temples of Stone   10
Stone Calendars   12
Stone Arrangements in Australia   15
North American Medicine Wheels   17
Stone Rows   19
Pillar and Boundary Stones   20
Sacred Powers   24
Basin Stones   26
Stone Altars   27
Healing Stones   29
Stones of Kingship   33
Spirit Stones   35
Spirit Portals   37
Fairy Lore   37
Dancing Circles   39
Reverence for Stones   41

Chapter 2: Stones and Energies   45

Geological Energies   46
Scientific Surveys   49
Art of Dowsing   49
Megaliths and Water   51
Bio-Electrical Charge   54
Stone Chakras   57
Geodetic Lines   57
Leys   58
Energies of Dolmen   59
Stone Circle Energies   61
Bora Grounds in Australia   64
Landscape Temples   66

Chapter 3: Megaliths and Petroglyphs   71
'Art' of the Petroglyphs   72
America's 'Ringing Rocks'   74
Australian Aboriginal Rock Rituals   75
Cosmological Petroglyphs   75
Cup Marks in Britain   78
Dowsing the Petroglyphs   79

Chapter 4: Creating Stone Arrangements   83
Stone Circle Revival   84
Small Circles for the Garden   85
Making Sacred Circles   89
Mini Stone Circles   89
Garden Miniliths   91
Making Medicine Wheels   94

Chapter 5: Labyrinths   97
Labyrinth Lore   98
Labyrinth Energies   103
Labyrinth Creation and Use   104
Labyrinth Rituals   108

Chapter 6: Working with Stones   113
Touchstones   114
Deviceless Dowsing   117
Tools for Geomancy   120
Stone Circle Medicine   122
Unwanted Effects   123
Healing of Sites   124
Stone Circle Rituals   125
Sacred Sites for Today   130

References   134
Python Press Books and Geomantica   137

Touchstone at the sacred centre of Castle Hill, an other-worldly landscape of weathered limestone karsts, in New Zealand's South Island.

Introduction

Ancient and enigmatic - Standing Stones, Labyrinths and Stone Circles still haunting various corners of the world have often been subject to systematic destruction. Yet, in some form, they have survived over several millennia. Their enduring presences beg so many questions. How did people manage to erect huge megalithic monuments, when it is a struggle to replicate them even today? For what purposes were they made? They must have been highly significant, given the enormous amount of effort involved. Science and folkore can provide clues. But personal experience of sites and energies detected at sacred stones can be much more revealing and rewarding than bland facts.

Sensitive people find that particular stones, both natural and intentionally placed, act as transmitters of beneficial natural energies, as well as anchor points for the power and spirit of the land. Not surprisingly, ancient traditions of healing, divination, wish fulfillment and fertility associated with certain sacred stones continue to find currency today. Anyone may potentially tune in to the sacred stones by taking up the ancient art of dowsing (also known as divining), or other forms of psychic attunement. It can be personally most enriching.

The purpose of this guidebook is to encourage people to discover for themselves the magical and transforming energies associated with both ancient megalithic sites and modern stones of power. And to be inspired to create one's own energetic stone arrangements, as Touchstones of interaction with the Sacred Earth.

Author Alanna Moore has been a geomancer for 30 years, sensing and advising on the energies and spirit of place. As a researcher and teacher of dowsing, she is uniquely placed to comprehend the vast subject of Earth Mysteries and to guide us in how this knowledge might be useful today. An advocate for promoting harmony in all the worlds, she invites you to join in this down-to-Earth journey of re-discovering and applying ancient wisdom in the everyday environment.

Chapter 1: Ancient Traditions

A stone circle in Cornwall, England.

Temples of Stone

Standing Stones, Circles of stone and other stone arrangements are found around the planet. In Britain there are some 900 Stone Circles that date from the European megalithic golden age, of about 4,000 BCE to 1,500 BCE. The tradition of erecting stone temples and monuments continued elsewhere until much later.

The world's densest concentration of megaliths is in Senegal/Gambia, in Africa, where there are over 1,000 stone circles. Around 29,000 iron worked laterite Standing Stones, ranging from 1 m (1.1 yd) to 2.5 m (2.7 yd) high, are located in an area some 100 km (65 ml) by 350 kms (218 ml), and centred around the Gambier River. In 2006 a selection were placed under World Heritage Listing. Erected in funerary rites around 1,500 years ago, today the local population has little knowledge of them.

In Europe, ancient megaliths inspired much fascination and speculation of the archeologists and antiquarians of the last few centuries. But it is only in the last hundred years or so that a wholistic appreciation of them has emerged. Folklore certainly helps to keep memories of them alive and provides intriguing clues to many of their mysteries.

The ancient megaliths were erected for a variety of purposes and come in various types of arrangements. Often of striking natural shape, colour or form, their timeless qualities and inherent powers must have fascinated the Neolithic peoples. The idea that many were temples concerned with the agricultural cycle of the year is hinted at by old tales associating them, Britain's Stonehenge for example, with bakers and loaves of bread. Stories speak of people trying to count the stones by placing loaves upon each one, but becoming befuddled in the process. This surely is a memory of votive offerings once given there, such as the tradition of offering the first loaf at the start of harvest, Lammas time ('loaf mass') in early August, when the northern autumn begins.

At the Grange Stone Circle at Lough Gur, near Limerick in Ireland, the main stone, representing Crom Dubh the dark Underworld god of agriculture (right), had legendary oracular powers and was garlanded with flower and fruit offerings given as thanks for a good harvest. The bones of oxen slain in sacrifice and feasted upon at the festival of Samhain, in early November when winter begins, have also been found in the circle.

With the demise of the native religion of the Earth, the great megalithic monuments languished, suffering centuries of wholesale destruction. They might have been doomed to being quarried out of existence, but fortunately British antiquarians John Aubrey, in the late 17th century and William Stukely in the early 18th century, rediscovered many megalithic sites and put them back into fashion. Interestingly, both these men were Freemasons, who no doubt had some knowledge of the ancient wisdoms, including sacred geometry, that are contained in the enduring stone monuments.

As for the large, solitary Standing Stones that the French dubbed Menhirs, these are also known as Pillar Stones. They are sometimes found to be actually remnants of destroyed Stone Circles. Stone Circles themselves are sometimes all that are left of a Dolmen structure. Also called Passage Graves and Passage Mounds, the Dolmen is the central stone chamber (see photo on page 60) surrounded by a circle of stones, correctly called kerbstones, that once edged a massive mound of earth that covered the whole structure.

True Stone Circles, Stonehenge and Avebury, in Wiltshire UK, are the greatest examples of Stone Henges. Henges were built of stone and also wood originally. The massive Henges were enclosed within huge earthen banks and have one or more entrances. Henges have no ditches around them, thus any encircling banks were more about sanctity than defence. They were temples to celebrate the cycles of life, with the Dolmens celebrating the cults of the dead and rebirth.

Below: A decorated kerbstone at the Knowth Passage Mound, near Newgrange, Ireland.

Calendars in Stone

Avebury is the largest known megalithic Henge in Europe. At some 5,700 years of age, it once consisted of 600 huge Standing Stones, the tallest of which has been known since historical times as The Obelisk. Within the main circle were two smaller Stone Circles, with a tradition of them being dedicated to the Sun and the Moon. Today only 76 of Avebury's stones are left standing, following wholesale destruction mainly in the last millenia. In the 1930's a certain amount of reconstruction was attempted of Avebury's fallen stones, with questionable accuracy at their reinstament.

At the beginning of the 20th century, eminent astronomer Sir Norman Lockyer intensely studied British Stone Circles for clues to them being used as astronomical observatories. He went on to find them purposefully positioned in particular alignments, often aligned with prominent landscape features and other markers visible in the vicinity, to enable observations of the movements of the Sun, Moon and other heavenly bodies. The whole landscape was thus involved in this calendrical function. Stone Circles were thus able to be used as calendars, foretelling times for seasonal agricultural duties and holy days. While his work took a long time to be accepted, Lockyer is now appreciated as the father of astro-archeology.

The scientific establishment at the time was greatly challenged with these notions, for it was generally presumed that Neolithic people were brutish and brainless. Science had become the new quasi-religious paradigm and the notion that the stone temples embodied an incredible amount of astronomical knowledge was akin to blasphemy. Many megalithic monuments involved awesome feats of engineering and a knowledge of Pythagorean geometry that was evident one thousand years before the time of Pythagoras. It was easier to just ignore the whole issue!

Stonehenge was one of the first to have its secrets revealed. At around 4,000 years of age (it's last phase of construction ending around 1,600 BCE), it is the best loved of British stone monuments. Stonehenge also has the most obvious astronomical alignments, Lockyer discovered. Today it is well understood that around June 21st the midsummer sun rises along the line of an axis that extends down the stone avenue at Stonehenge, with the midwinter sun setting in exactly the opposite

direction around December 21st. Both of these events can be viewed from the centre of the circle through narrow stone portals. (This had already been revealed by John Aubrey.) The Station Stones were found to mark May Day sunset, plus sunrise on November 1st.

As at other megalithic sites studied, Lockyer noted that the earliest of megalithic sites (or the earliest parts of sites) marked the all-important festival dates on the cross quarter days, the mid points between the summer and winter solstice times that heralded the new seasons. These were at the beginning of February, May, August and November, and they were considered to be portal-like points of time of great mythic import. Lough Gur's Grange Circle has a stone avenue alignment to the early August Lughnasadh/Lammas festival, as well as to Samhain, in early November.

At later sites, or in later reconstructions at existing sites, the emphasis had shifted more to the solar solstice dates, Lockyer found. This may well signify a shift from more Earth based pagan religion to one of solar deity supremacy. It probably signified the arrival in the British Isles of the great sun god Lugh, with a wave of immigrant Celtic people coming from the continent. Before those times, Goddesses ruled together with Gods and the Earth's fecundity was honoured as absolutely fundamental to life, with Underworld forces pre-eminent.

It took some six decades after Lockyer before astro-archeology rattled orthodox scientific thought again. American astronomy Professor Gerald Hawkins published his studies of Stonehenge in the prestigious journal *Nature* in 1963. Hawkins spoke about the numerous sighting lines and stone alignments there that point to solar and lunar azimuths. He deduced that the 56 Aubrey holes that ring the main megalithic complex had been intended to mark the 56 years taken by the moon to complete its eclipse cycle - being three nodal revolutions each of 18.61 years length. The Aubrey holes could thus be used to predict lunar eclipses. These can be treacherous times, when earthquakes, volcanic eruptions, high tides and wild weather are more prevalent, and it can be dangerous for transplanting seedlings or sowing seeds.

An unique example of a small Stone Circle, located not far from Sydney, and said to have been a ritual site once used for men's initiation.

Stone Arrangements in Australia

Australian Aboriginals in rocky areas occasionally made stone arrangements and it was the principle form of artistic expression in the state of Victoria. The largest concentration of Standing Stones is thought to be at Murujuga, also known as the Burrup Peninsula on the north coast of Western Australia, which includes tall standing stones similar to the European Menhirs, as well as circular stone arrangements.

Today the idea of ancient megalithic sites in Europe and elsewhere as being cosmic observatories is common knowledge. But the idea that Australian Aboriginal people were also building stone arrangements with astronomical alignments was unheard of until recent years. In 2009 Ray Norris, a British astrophysicist working for the CSIRO, Australia's national science agency, was able to confirm that Wurdi Youang, a Wathaurong Aboriginal Stone 'Circle', unique in Victoria, is most likely an intentionally designed stone arrangement marking solstice and equinox sun set positions, as originally proposed by astro-archeologist John Morieson.

Set on an undulating basalt plain north of the You Yang hills, near to the township of Little River, the site consists of a 50 m (55 yd) diameter ovate stone arrangement, its major axis aligned almost exactly east-west. It comprises up to 100 blocks of basalt, weighing on average 90 kg (200 lb) and one around 500 kg (half a ton), the tallest rising 75 cm (2.5 ft) from the ground. Some rocks are positioned on the bare bedrock, but most are firmly dug into the ground, with 22 having rock wedges under them inserted for stability. With a total weight of some 23 tonnes of rock positioned on a site that slopes 3 m (3.2 yd) down towards the Little River, it was a substantial effort to build!

Nearby, a headland above the river valley was found to have ample evidence of Wathaurong occupation, and also nearby, stone fish traps have been found on the river, suggesting a place of food abundance, perfect for gatherings. Barely known before an article about it was published in the *Records of the Victorian Archeological Survey* in June 1980, the site is of unknown age.

Aboriginal calendars were often quite complex, with up to six seasons. The appearance of certain stars often told of the onset of a new season. For example - *"Pitjantjatjara people say that the rising of the Pleiades in the dawn sky in May heralds the start of winter"*, says Norris.

Norris believes that people here were watching for the longest and shortest days of the year, and the equinoctal midway points, possibly to

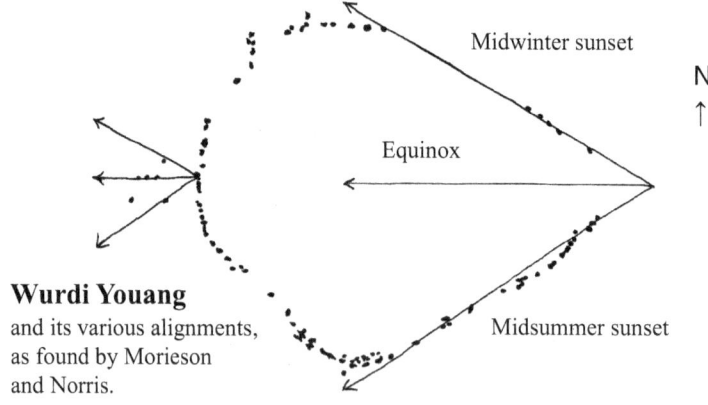

Wurdi Youang and its various alignments, as found by Morieson and Norris.

inform their seasonal movements around territory. The Aboriginal presence in this region goes back at least 27,000 years, Norris points out. "[John] Morieson (2003) suggested that three small outlying stones (the 'outliers') marked the setting sun at the solstices and equinoxes when viewed from three very prominent stones at the western apex," he said. "*We have shown that the Morieson hypothesis is supported, in that the azimuths over the outliers do indeed indicate the position of the setting Sun on the equinoxes and solstices, and that the probability of this occurring by chance is low (about 0.25%),*"

Aboriginal stone arrangement, a pair of small Stone Circles, in northern NSW, now relocated to Heritage Park, Mullumbimby.

he wrote. "*Additionally, we found that the straight sides of the arrangement also indicate the solstices while the three prominent stones at the western apex of the arrangement mark the point where the sun sets at equinox. [Thus] we can say with relative confidence that these alignments were intentional.*"

Morieson also considers Wurdi Youang's shape/outline to be possibly that of an abalone and symbolic of female genitalia. "*To me it's obviously a Dreaming place,*" he told me. The site lies on Wathaurong Co-Operative land and may one day be available for public viewing.

North American Medicine Wheels

A variation of the Stone Circle, the Medicine Wheel is sacred to native American people. A good example, and the most well known one, is

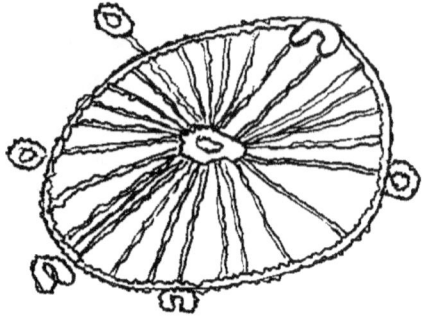

the Big Horn Medicine Wheel, near Sheridan in north Wyoming (as above). This spiderweb like stone arrangement sits high on the shoulder of the sacred Medicine Mountain, one of the Big Horn Mountains. It consists of an imperfect circle of large boulders with a diameter of around 25 m (82 ft). There is a central rock cairn 3.6 m (12 ft) across and 60 cm (2 ft) high, from which 28 'spokes' - unevenly placed lines of smaller stones - radiate out to the 'rim' of the wheel. Around the rim are six stone cairns placed at irregular intervals.

The significance of the 28 spokes pays homage to the lunar month of 28 days. When building special teepees, 28 wooden struts are used in the construction of the Oglala Sioux Medicine Lodges.

Astro-archeological studies of alignments there find that one of the spokes is oriented to summer solstice sunrise and sunset, a time of midsummer rituals for local tribal people and time for the Sun Dance.

There are other alignments, such as from the cairns to prominent landscape features in the surrounding horizon, towards the stars Aldebaran, Rigel and Sirius, whose risings heralded festival days. Curiously, these stars rise heliacally 28 days apart, with Aldebaran starting to rise at the summer solstice from 1400 AD onwards.

The same sorts of alignments are found in the Moose Mountain Medicine Wheel in Saskatchewan, Canada, although it only has five spokes and may be a thousand years older. So Medicine Wheels also had calendrical function, just like Stone Circles across the Atlantic.

Stone Rows

In Europe, massive freestanding Menhirs are sometimes found erected in grand rows or avenues (double rows). Triple rows are also found, but rarely. Across the once fertile area of Dartmoor are found around 62 Stone Rows, ranging from 15 m (50 ft) long to some 3.2 km (2 miles).

Usually in straight or curved lines, they were sometimes erected as wavy lines, as at the megalithic site at Carnac in Brittany, France, where many of Carnac's stones weigh over 50 tonnes each! Here eleven wavy stone rows snake their way across the landscape.

At Stonehenge the remains of a mighty stone avenue enters the Circle at the Heel Stone (below). Rising some 4.8 m (16 ft) high, this Menhir stands outside the main monument and is itself encircled by a small ditch. It marks a solar alignment from the central Altar Stone towards sunrise on midsummers day.

The Henge at Avebury once boasted two grand avenues comprised of around 100 pairs of stones. These stone pairs faced each other, with one side of the avenue having only tall masculine type Pillar Stones, the other side with more squat, rounded shaped megaliths. Yang balancing yin.

People once walked ceremonially down along the outside of the avenue towards the Henge. At the other end of one of the rows was the Stone Circle now known as The Sanctuary. Today only one forlorn Menhir remains of what once was a 40 m (130 ft) diameter Stone Circle that also had a smaller circle inside of it.

Pillar and Boundary Stones

Solitary Menhirs, those often antenna or phallic shaped standing stones, nowadays called Pillar Stones, are a common relic of the megalithic era. Globally, it was once customary to place Pillar Stones as boundary markers. The Celtic tribes of Europe also installed a significant Pillar Stone, an omphalos, to mark the centre of their teritory. It was usually phallic or dome shaped.

The tallest Pillar Stone in Ireland is the Long Stone, of Punchestown, County Kildare. At 7 m (23ft) tall, this slender stone is typical of the Bronze Age.

During Ireland's Iron Age, Pillar Stones (such as on the right) were often erected to commemorate the dead. They were sometimes inscribed with the proto-writing Ogham, a series of dashes grooved into the edges of the stones. Surviving into the Christian era, some Irish Pillar Stones were later reconsecrated to the local saint, with a cross carved into them.

Pairs of Pillar Stones may be found too. One is typically tall and thin; the other small, square and blunt topped. These yang/yin pairs were believed to function as gateways to sacred precincts, as in the legend of that well known Irish couple, called Blocc and Bluigne (seen next page). This pair of stones, standing at the entrance to the royal Hill of Tara, were involved with the rituals of sacred kingship. Legends tell

that the king-to-be had to drive his chariot at the pair and the stones would allow a rightful king easy passage between them, but others would be denied access. A small *sheela-na-gig* (Earth Goddess) figure is carved into the taller stone.

In Italy, Numa, the first king of Rome after Romulus, was said to have divided up the land and installed *termini* stones at its boundaries to mark territory. These special stones were dedicated to Jupiter and it was a capital offense to interfere with them. Over in Greece, stone pillars marking territory were called *hermae*.

Boundary Stones in ancient Babylonia were elaborately carved with fabulous relief designs. These *Kudurru* monuments provided vivid and permanent records of land ownership and privileges, such as tax exemptions in the Kaassite period. Their penis head like form probably harks back to an earlier era of being agricultural field markers. As important legal documents, they were later stored in temples for safe keeping.

One Kudurru (seen next page) depicts the Sun, Moon and Venus at the top, symbolizing major Mesopotamian deities Shamash, Sin and Ishtar, as they witness and guarantee the legal grant of land. Other symbols refer to other gods, altars, divine creatures and celestial powers, with some being precursors of the signs of the zodiac.

In Britain, ceremonies of Beating the Bounds involved ritual perambulations around parish boundaries and often wild beating of the Boundary Stones with hazel rods. In Cornwall an old stone boundary marker that had been fashioned with a rough cross on top in later times was visited annually. Pilgrims would dig up some earth from around the base of this old Pillar Stone, then toss it up into the air and all over it, probably in memory of some older agricultural ritual.

Touchstones for Today

Above - Babylonian Kudurra Boundary Stone, British Museum.
Top right - Swedish Boundary Stone, Stockholm Museum.
Bottom right: Swedish commemorative stone on a rural roadside.

Pillar and Boundary Stones

Sacred Powers

Particular stones have long been revered for exuding beneficial powers. Certain Menhirs have been associated with the maintenance of regional Earth harmony, for example. If stones were destroyed, people feared crop failure and this has indeed occurred. When stones were re-instated, things have got back to normal, with harmony restored and crops growing healthily again.

Even as late as 1944 this has occurred. In that year in Essex, England some American air force men moved a Menhir that in legend marked the grave of a witch. Straight afterwards the effects began to be felt in the district: cows' milk dried up, hens stopped laying eggs, haystacks fell over and the church bell started to ring of its own accord. Life only returned to normal when the stone was replaced!

Stones have long been associated with the fertility of the land and also that of animals and people. Couples once visited stones to make their marriage vows, when they wished for children or an easy birth. Rites often involved touching special stones, putting hands through holes in stones or holding hands around them, or sitting on top of them.

The eternal quality of stones made some popular for oath taking up until the early 19th century. The Odin Stone, a Holed Stone in Orkney, that was destroyed by a farmer in 1814, was one such stone. Promises made to Odin, that is, oaths sworn on that stone, were considered legally binding. It was the custom to leave offerings of some bread, cheese or cloth at the stone as a gesture of thanks.

Other Menhirs were visited for invoking good weather by fishermen and sailors. For example - ancient Dolmen stones of the Channel Islands were described in 16th and 17th century manuscripts as '*altars of the Gods of the sea.*' Many a Menhir was visited there regularly, as a place to honour the ancient deities and pray for safe conditions.

In Scotland, the Kempock Stane, or Granny Kempock, is a 2.1 m (7 ft) high Menhir that overlooks the Clyde estuary, near Gourock. To this stone fishermen once brought gifts and baskets of sand from the seaside. They would walk around it several times sprinkling sand at its base, while asking for good weather and a large catch of fish. One may presume that Granny Kempock was originally a Goddess of the sea.

Others stones were used for granting wishes, especially considering the ancient belief that good luck could be garnered by maintaining the good will of the spirits of place. Often certain Menhirs would sadly shrink over time, from so many people chipping off a little piece to take home as a good luck souvenir!

Resplendent with an array of gifts, the stone of Cailleach Bhearra (the Old Hag Goddess) at Kilcatherine, Co. Cork Ireland, looks out over the waters towards her sea god lover (below). Covered with trinkets, feathers, pebbles and other offerings, she is well frequented to this day and is a popular wishing stone.

Basin Stones

Basin Stones are the name for certain Menhirs, including many natural boulders, that have basin-like depressions carved into them. The circular basins are usually found on the upper side of recumbent stones (that lie horizontally on the ground). In Ireland they are called *Bullauns*. The largest basins are usually no wider than 90 cm (3 ft) across and 7.6 cm (3 in) deep. They are often positioned to collect rain and dew from the rock surface, with a channel to take away surplus water.

To appease the local spirits of place, offerings of food, water or milk were once made in the hollows of Basin Stones. In Scotland these *Dobby Stanes* were where offerings of milk were given to please the wild female spirit of the pastures, the Gruagach. In the Scottish highlands the Stone of the Long Haired One (Clach na Gruagach) at Gairloch had offerings of milk given to the Gruagach daily, in a tradition that continued right up to the early 20th century. Should the dairy maids neglect to do this, trouble would always follow!

Some Basin Stones in coastal areas were used for rites in the raising or soothing of winds. Offerings were placed by fishermen in the basin in the direction that the wind was required to blow from.

Many of the Irish Bullauns were probably originally used for the communal grinding of sacred cakes for harvest rituals. Perhaps that's why they are often found with their basins holding large rounded pebbles, not unlike old grinding stones. Tthey are often found located in ancient fair grounds, where the harvest festival was celebrated by the people of the land. (Read more on this subject in my book *Sensitive Permaculture*.)

St Bridgit's 'Cursing Stones', a mossy Bullaun in an old churchyard at Killinagh, Co. Cavan, Ireland.

Stone Altars

Later, in Christian times, the Bullauns and round stones in them were considered to be objects for magical working and associated with witchcraft. A good example is found in a quiet backwater of Ireland, where St Bridget's 'Cursing Stone' at Killinagh, Co. Cavan, overlooks Upper Lough MacNean. It has also been called St Bridgets Wishing Chair. The author clairvoyantly observed nine witchy spirits encircling this Bullaun, they appeared to be acting as guardians of the site.

Though the term Cursing Stone was used by the old scholars to describe such rocks, in popular parlance they were more often known as Blessing Stones. With the native Irish stone magic, one could wish for good or bad to happen! A clockwise turning of the round stones could invoke healing and good luck; while turning them widdershins (anti-clockwise) could effect a curse. (But a wrongly sent curse was considered to rebound on the curser.)

Sometimes spiritual preparation was required before using such Blessing Stones. People would often fast, then make pilgrimage to the old sacred sites that had been nominally Christianised. Here they recited prayers (sometimes walking backwards while reciting them) and turned the stones according to their whim, in order to release their power.

At the holy island of Iona, where Irish monks established a monastic centre of learning, there is a prominent Basin Stone at an ancient ruined church altar. In it's basins round stones were traditionally turned around clockwise by pilgrims to ensure good luck.

In Ireland a surprising number of Stone Altars have also survived in quiet backwaters (as on the cover of this book). These drystone tables with large rounded pebbles, called *leachta* in Irish, are usually located in association with holy wells, ancient churchyards and Sacred Sites.

The most famous Stone Altar in Ireland is on Inishmurray, an island off the west coast. The Speckled Stones are about seventy rounded, water-washed stones, some carved with crosses on them, sitting on a drystone altar within the old monastic enclosure, that lies in ruins around it. The last and most celebrated time this Stone Altar was used was in the 1940s, when the ritual was successfully worked to curse Adolf Hitler during World War Two.

Apparently Ireland's early saints were not shy to do the odd bit of cursing themselves, having read in their Old Testament of Moses and Elijah building altars of stone to curse the enemies of Christianity.

The author tunes into a sacred Stone Altar amidst churchyard ruins near Carrick-on-Shannon, County Leitrim, Ireland.

Healing Stones

Global traditions attest that certain stones can transfer healing energies to people, both directly and via the medium of water. People once collected and drank the energised dew that ran off Healing Stones, imprinted with their special energy. The Basin Stones of Stonehenge are good examples, and they were once regarded with the highest esteem. Geoffrey of Monmouth wrote of Stonehenge that: *"in these stones is a mystery, and a healing virtue against many ailments....they did wash the stones and pour forth the water into the baths, whereby they that were sick were made whole. Moreover they did mix confections of herbs with the water, whereby they that were wounded had healing, for not a stone is there that lacketh in virtue of leechcraft."*

Many Bullauns were associated with the power of healing, also via the water that collected in them. They were especially popular for eye complaints and wart removal. (In the typically smoky households, eye problems were rife.)

In other traditions, direct contact with stones was often the method used. From India to Europe there are many examples of Healing Holed Stones - rocks with formed or natural holes through which people squeezed, in the quest for a cure for backache, rheumatism, or for general regeneration; or placed their hands through (see page 132).

Men an Tol is the most famous of Healing Holed Stones in Britain. The three stones were possibly the remnants of a Neolithic burial chamber or Dolmen, that may have also been aligned to the May Day sunrise. The largest stone has a round hole in it some 60 cm (2ft) in diameter, through which sickly children (in particular, those with rickets) were once passed for a cure. The stones, which are not in their original positions, were also used in the prevention and cure of various illnesses of a rheumatic nature. A series of ritual activities once popularly undertaken there included crawling, or being passed through the hole three or nine times anti-clockwise. Sometimes children were also drawn along the grass in an easterly direction. The stones were also used for divination, with visitors bringing brass pins that they placed on top of the stones. A modern replica of Men an Tol, erected in Cornwall on private property not far from the original stones, is visited by many people who crawl through it for backache cures to this day.

Stone Seats were also used. Sometimes naturally formed in rock outcrops, others have been shaped deliberately. St Fillans Chair is a seat in natural rock on Dunfillan hill in Perthshire, Scotland, that became famed as a cure for rheumatism. One climbed up the rocks to the chair, sat in it, and then was pulled down the hillside by the ankles!

Stone Beds were once slept upon to gain cures, such as for epilepsy, and also to aid conception and birth. The Irish called them Saint's Beds to give them an aura of Christianity! The principle of the incubation of the spirit for transformation and renewal was invoked by sleeping a night or two upon the Stone Beds. In more recent traditions it was deemed enough to simply lie in them for a short time and to turn oneself over, ideally, three times.

Stone Altars often retain ancient healing traditions. The author met an elderly woman in a quiet corner of County Leitrim at St Ronan's Altar, next to St Laissar's Holy Well, an old pilgrimage site. The woman explained how her backache had been cured in her youth (70 years before) by crawling beneath the stone table there. It's big round single pebble looked clean and new, and I imagine that the site's artefacts have been renewed over time, as required.

Sometimes very small stones held legendary healing powers. Portable healing stones were often unusual specimens, such as fine quartz crystals, or strangely shaped rocks and fossils. They might have been

Healing Stones

taken home by the ailing, or put into water to charge it up with healing powers. Such minilithic stones may also look fairly ordinary. The Straining Threads, located in an old churchyard in Killerry, Co. Sligo, Ireland is an example, however there is nothing ordinary about them!

Old bits of string were wound around the main, peg-like stone, as seen below. People with various ailments traditionally came here and took some of the thread which they rubbed onto afflicted parts for a cure. If you couldn't come yourself, a friend would bring a piece of unbleached linen thread and wind it around the main stone. The other stones were then each turned sunwise, while a prayer was recited. An old thread from a previous visitor was then removed and brought to the distant patient and bound around the affected part for a cure.

Another out-of-the-way ancient Irish site, St Attracta's Well near Monasteraden in County Sligo, is named for a fifth century saint. The mysterious row of large rounded pebbles along the back wall of the Well there were once visited and handled to gain cures for warts, rickets and other common ailments. When women wanted to conceive they would take one home for a while. No wonder they are still referred to as Serpent Stones and that the church has put a dampener on this practice! The stones are today firmly embedded into the wall.

Stones of Kingship

Certain Menhirs became enduring monuments for the inauguration of kings and chieftains, who would stand or sit upon them as symbolic of their own potency. In Britain the most famous is the 'Stone of Scone' (or 'of Destiny'), a 200 kg (450 lb) block of red sandstone kept beneath the throne. Thirty four Scottish kings were enthoned upon it, before Edward 1 of England seized it and in 1296 it was removed from Scone, Perthshire, and brought to the Houses of Parliament at Westminster. Here a special oaken chair was made for it. The stone, now back in Scotland, will be borrowed back when the next English monarch is crowned.

In Ireland another Stone of Destiny (*Lia Fail,* seen on the right), located on the royal Hill of Tara is a classic inauguration stone of an even older lineage. The phallic shaped Pillar Stone is said to roar or shriek out loudly when the true, legitimate king is to be crowned.

Another omphalos is the dome shaped 1 m (3.3 ft) high granite Turoe Stone in County Galway. The finest of Ireland's five royal ritual stones, the group are decoratively carved in the Iron Age curvilinear La Tene style. The Castlestrange Stone, located near Athleague in Roscommon, is another fabulous example (seen next page). With their beautiful carvings, these wonderful stones are thought to be associated with the inauguration ceremonies of chiefs, conveying sacred kingship over the land. An axis mundi for territory, the would-be king was symbolically united with the Goddess of the land through them, in order to gain legitimacy of rule.

Such sacred stones could infuse the sitter with the power to command, both physically and psychically. Stone Seats were also used as potent sites for conferring authority and associated with the powerful people of their times - the druids, saints or chieftains and kings. (They were probably the seats of important landscape spirits, as well.)

Footprints carved into natural stone were also once closely associated with kingship in northern Europe. At the crowning moment of kingship rituals in ancient Pictish Scotland, the king-to-be thrust his foot into the stone print. In this symbolic act the Goddess of the land became the royal foot holder.

In Cornwall Stone Circles were used for coronations up until the 14th century. The king would stand at the centre stone and his noblemen would be stationed around him adjacent to their own representative stones. This circular arrangement was similar to that of royal rituals of the Irish kings at Tara.

Spirit Stones

Shinto, the ancient animist tradition of Japan, has long recognised rocks as the homes of the *kami*, spirit beings of the Earth. Stones acting as special seats of important landscape devas are called *iwakura*. Similar traditions are found universally, although typically they have been suppressed and fragmented by modern religion.

Malaysian roadside Spirit House, used to honour the spirits of nature.

Spirit shrines with special stones in them, as in the photos, are ubiquitous across Asia and many other parts of the world.

Ancient Greek philosophers described how spiritual deities may be attracted to stones and stone effigies by using ritual, and that regular acts of reverence would cause them to take up residence there. That stones really can act as portals and anchor points for a range of spirits, from the great deities of the Earth, to the lesser spirits of nature, is confirmed today by sensitives and dowsers.

In modern Theosophical literature (derived from ancient Indian mystical wisdom) the nature spirit beings belong to other-dimensional kingdoms, existing on the *etheric, astral* and other frequencies of energy and exhibited consciousness and intelligence. Following the Indian view, one might collectively call them the *devas*, from the original Sanskrit word, meaning 'shining ones'. The devas are often perceived in the form of lights.

Whatever form they choose to make (and the astral realm is very fluid), the devas have varying levels of intelligence and feelings. Their emotional aspects, as vibrations in the astral realm, can pervade a place and be palpable to many people who go there. If the devas are happy, then their happy energy will permeate the space around them and help to make all beings there feel good. If they wish to communicate with humans, they can project 'thought-forms' of images, also feelings or sounds. In one's own garden, giving them a special Stone Seat, or Spirit House, as a deva station, is a very good idea!

Below: Another Spirit House in Malaysia. This one in a shop features a stone cobra, surrounded by offerings of water and incense.

Spirit Portals

Natural rock surfaces, especially cracks and fissures, have long been regarded as entrances to the spirit world and emergence places for the devas. Thus shamen in trance states would go into rock faces to commune with the spirit world. In Ontario, Canada, for example, gifted shamen were said to have the power to go inside cliff faces to meet with spirits and exchange 'good medicine', tobacco for supernatural power.

Do you have to be a shaman to go into a rock? No, it turns out. I've heard of this happening on a more casual basis in recent times, at one of the planet's most sacred sites - Uluru (also known as Ayers Rock) in central Australia. Billy Arnold reported hearing astonishing, parallel stories from two women in Alice Springs, told to him separately at different times. Both were visitors, one American, who had felt drawn irresistably to make the journey to that enormous red rock, iconic Uluru.

Upon entering a particular sacred women's cave in the side of Uluru, the women had been transported into another dimension. They reported being greeted by a group of Aboriginal women elders - in spirit - coming to them in the cave and inviting them to go with them inside the rock, which they did. What happened when they went inside I do not know, but I'd say that they were incredibly privileged to receive such a spiritual awakening into the Dreamtime dimensions. I'm sure that they felt blessed also. Those spirit elderwomen had been initiating Aboriginal women into life's mysteries for a long time, and I guess they still relish opportunities to enlighten women, particularly those who come to them with open minds and hearts.

Fairy Lore

Over in Europe, it was also recognised that certain significant stones were gateways to Fairyland. In a Welsh tale, a lost shepherd boy was taken into Fairyland at a certain Menhir in the mountains. The mysterious old man who took him there tapped three times on the stone, which then lifted up to reveal a stairway going down into the Underworld. Going down the stairs, the boy went on to take up residence in the fertile land of the Fair Folk.

Special Fairy Stones were not always significant landmarks. A Catholic priest interviewed by Evans Wentz explained the enduring belief that *"a heap of stones in a field should not be disturbed, though needed for building - especially if they are part of an ancient tumulus. The fairies are said to live inside the pile and to move the stones would be most unfortunate."*

Many a Stone Circle has been associated with legends of resident fairy beings and dragon spirits. In some cases light phenomena, called 'fairy lights', have been observed at sites by various witnesses. In modern sightings these have sometimes been interpreted as UFO activity; but it is just as likely to be Earth energy phenomena, I feel.

Of Carnac's megaliths, in the early 1900's researcher Evans-Wentz was told that its resident fairies had the power to turn mortal men into stone. Of Cornwall's Men-an-Tol, he was told by an old local that there *"is supposed to be a fairy guardian or pixy* [there] *who can make miraculous cures"*. These are reminders of earlier times when the genius loci of the site was recognised as being in charge of the energies of place and of dispensing cures or curses.

Irish fairy stories are a rich treasure of ancient lore, more records of real encounters between people and The Gentry (as nature spirits were sometimes called), than fantasy tales. Many are not that old either. When the stories were collected (largely in the late 19th century) they were often current tales of encounters between the devas and friends and relatives of the people interviewed.

Cornwall has its Spriggans, one of five 'species' recognised there, wrote Robert Pope, in the early 19th century. These are spirits *"found only about the cairns, quoits or cromlechs, barrows or detached stones, with which it is unlucky for humans to meddle. They are a remarkably mischevous and thievish tribe,"* he said. Indeed warning tales crop up everywhere about not disturbing sacred sites and the retribution wrought by cranky sprites for doing so. Such beings are the guardian spirits, whose presence and the people's respect for them has preserved many a megalithic site from desecration over the millenia.

That we offend the devas and destroy their homes at our peril, is the theme of many a fairy story. Real live fairies are not all sweetness and light, they have ample capacity to annoy humans if disturbed, potentially using hypnotic suggestion or psychic attack to make life unbearable for the desecrators.

Dancing Circles

European traditions go that the most popular past time for Stone Circle fairies was that of circle dancing. Fairies, in one example, were said to regularly dance around the King Stone of the Rollright Stone Circle group, having emerged from a hole in the bank nearby.

People were once enthusiastic circle dancers inside the Stone Circles, as well. And circular dancing at Sacred Sites, such as the corroborrees of Australian Aboriginals in their Bora Grounds, is practiced globally. Writing a century ago in Britain, E.M. Nelson described how naked men and women once ran nine times around Stone Circles, in what he suggested must have been part of a fertility rite. (The number nine often comes up at Stone Circles. It could hark back to the triple Goddess of the old religions. Her three aspects can also be triple.)

Such accounts were anathema to the Church! Legends from Christian times have it that certain circles were previously dancers turned to stone in punishment for their pagan practises. Usually their crime was to have had too much fun on the sabbath day or eve. In Cornwall, near Lamorna, the Merry Maidens Stone Circle is said to be a group of girls who, walking in the fields one sabbath evening, became entranced by fairy music made by a couple of spirit pipers, and began to dance. But they were struck by a lightning flash and turned to stone. The two pipers were also thus struck and they are now a couple of Menhirs in a nearby field. The Nine Maidens (also known as Boscawen-un), in Devon, were also said to have been petrified for dancing on Sunday; the stones themselves are said to dance each day at noon! There are many other examples and even Stonehenge was once called The Giants Dance.

However the legends of petrified dancers were only written down from the 17th and 18th centuries, Christine Zucchelli points out. Before then, popular belief associated the Stone Circles with dancing fairies, not humans. It wasn't the first time that new religions re-interpreted and re-told old legends to suit their own agendas.

Why did people dance within the Stone Circles? As well as having lots of fun, they probably accessed trance states this way, the rhythmic circle dancing having a hypnotic effect. Ancient initiation and fertility rites probably involved singing and dancing, and they would have helped to joyously bond the clans people together in an ecstatic state. Dowser researcher Tom Lethbridge also pointed out that - *"by means of exciting people to execute wild circular dances, power could be generated and stored in stones and trees."*

But was it just people and devas who did the dancing? When Lethbridge tried to date a stone at the Merry Maidens by pendulum dowsing, he was surprised and literally shocked, he wrote in *The Legend of the Sons of God*.

"The hand resting on the stone received a strong tingling sensation like a mild electric shock and the pendulum itself shot out until it was circling nearly horizontally to the ground. The stone itself, which must have weighed over a ton, felt as if it were rocking and almost dancing about," he said. When English dowser and author Tom Graves investigated certain Menhirs in modern times it was as if the stones were dancing to his sensitive touch. *"Traditions of 'dancing stones' suddenly became tangible reality,"* he wrote, in *Elements of Pendulum Dowsing*.

Reverence for Stones

The magical Menhirs attracted all manner of reverence in times past. Well into the 19th century people still clung fast to their ancestral traditions and thus the enduring stones greatly antagonised the Church. Catholics were able to absorb some of the megalithic sites in hybrid traditions, but for the Protestants, the mystical megaliths were way too pagan! Some they set to and 'converted', re-carving them into church and market crosses.

Some of the ancient Menhirs were stations for earthy agricultural deities and they were popular places for offerings to garner good crops. Other traditions saw particular stones honoured on pilgrimage days or visited in times of drought or famine. One English bluestone megalith in Lincolnshire, Boundels Stone, had a reputation for making rain, but first it had to be hit with hazel rods. Another stone nearby, Grim's Stone, when beaten, could make the corn grow big and people held an annual feast around the pair, which would be whipped *"till iverybody went wicked wi' prosperity."*

On the island of Guernsey people once made sacred processions to principal megalithic sites, round which *"the whole body of pilgrims solemnly revolved three times from east to west,"* Evans-Wenz noted. Also in Guernsey is found a much revered effigy stone which must have once represented a Goddess of Earthly fertility. Known as the Gran'mere du Chimquiere, this female figure used to be honoured with offerings of fruit and flowers, in order to gain good luck and fertility.

Nature religion didn't just feature Eath Mother Goddesses, there were many Earth Gods as well. Pillar Stones are often phallus shaped, honouring the masculine side of nature and also symbolic of good luck and fertility. But the Gods were even more suppressed by the Church than divine female figures.

A good example is the great stone of Irish agricultural God Crom Dubh that presides over the Grange Stone Circle at Lough Gur, Limerick. It was annually garlanded with fruit and flowers to give thanks for the harvest and ensure continuing fecundity of the land. The mighty stone was also revered for its oracular powers, that are still evident today, some people attest. However Crom Dubh himself is barely remembered at all, a victim of Christian spin doctors, who, at their best, described him, in the tales of the fictional life of St Patrick, as a generous landord, or, at worst, as a demonic Bull God.

Above: Peter Cowman adds to the coin pile on a concrete block altar beside Crom Dubh's Stone at the Grange Stone Circle in Limerick.

In Scotland the Bowing Stone, on the Isle of Skye, commanded tremendous respect. People wishing for a good harvest would walk around the stone three times and bow to it, as their ancestors had always done. So potent was the respect for it, that when a disapproving Church minister had the Bowing Stone torn down, people still bowed to it. It was tossed into a field and the farmer got annoyed at having his crops trampelled by visitors. Even after being broken up and dropped down a ravine, it was still bowed to. Finally a sheriff ordered it restored and so all remaining bits were collected together and piled up, and folk again came and continued to bow - setting fine examples of the strong connection to the land by its indigenous people.

Despite this deeply ingrained reverence for the sacred Earth, so many megalithic sites have been deliberately and systematically destroyed. We are left to feel the pain of the broken stone monuments that are but a shadow of their former grandeur. Fortunately today, what is left of Europe's Sacred Sites and megaliths, and even the natural haunts of the Little People, are protected by EU heritage laws. But statutary protection doesn't always work out well and archeology and tourism can destroy places in many ways. Locking sites away like museum pieces isn't very popular either!

We can consider megalithic ritual centres as windows to Earth's Dreaming dimension, potentially accessible to all. Their sacred stones as Touchstones for today. (If we are allowed to touch them!)

People are also now forging joyful connections to Country by creating their own sacred sites and interacting with special stones placed at power centres, following eco-sacred paradigms that are the rich heritage of all humanity.

Chapter 2: Stones and Energies

The Cheesering, a revered natural rock formation in Cornwall, England.

Geological Energies

In Britain the megalithic sites are often found in rocky and highly energetic places. In fact 80% of Britains 900 or so Stone Circles are built within a mile of a geological fault line, where Earth energies, such as gamma rays, are strong. UFO sightings are more common in these areas too. Individual stones are often found associated with localised magnetic anomalies, while in France most of the megalithic sites there are found in areas rich in uranium.

Not surprisingly, underlying geology has a lot to do with a site's energetic make-up, it's *feng shui*. Dowser researcher Guy Underwood declared that a majority of Sacred Sites in the UK are located where the underlying rock strata is usually limestone and chalk. These are very soft types of rock and, with enough water moving through them, they erode easily and develop numerous underground cavities and crevices.

The megalith builders sought out hard, durable rocks for their monuments, sometimes bringing them from long distances. Granite, which is slightly radioactive and often highly crystalline with a large percentage of quartz, was a popular choice for the megaliths.

Pure quartz was also a favourite. With its strong piezo-electrical ability, quartz can transform energies, often in a crackling flash. When squeezed, it can produce an electric current. This helps to explain some mystery light effects seen occasionally at particular sites. Rich in silica, quartz is diamagnetic, that is - weakly repulsed from a magnet.

Over the aeons quartz crystal has been universally revered as a power stone for divination and healing, in pieces ranging from great white quartz Menhirs down to small pocket-sized specimens. Irish people once placed small pieces of white quartz, called 'godstones', in graves.

Next page top: Victoria's last remaining Quartz Mountain, that somehow escaped destruction by gold mining, is located in the Paddy's Ranges, near Maryborough. Below: The Organ Pipes, near Melbourne, are classic basalt columns, formed when volcanic magma cools slowly under a surface layer of lava.

Geological Energies

Volcanic rock, such as basalt, was popular too. Basalt is paramagnetic, that is - weakly attracted to a magnet. Professor Phil Callahan noticed that paramagnetic rocks were often used in Ireland's Round Towers, which rise up 34 m (100 ft) into the sky. He discovered that these circa 1,000 year old *"silicon rich semi-conductors of energy"* were acting as huge antennas, waveguides that collect stimulating energies from the cosmos and send them down into the soil. The result can be a lush and healthy plant growth environment, supported by the Tower's strong magnetic field. No wonder the old bluestone monuments were often associated with fertility!

(The author has written extensively on the subject of paramagnetic rock in *Stone Age Farming*.)

Above: The Round Tower at Killala, County Mayo, Ireland, with a plan of its original situation, in an early Christian monastic complex, below.

Scientific Surveys

In order to unravel the mysteries of the sacred stones, the Dragon Project team have monitored, with scientific instruments, various energies at megaliths in the UK. Mostly focussing on the Rollright Stones, since the 1980's they have used gaussmeters (for magnetism), infrared cameras, ultrasonic detectors and geiger counters, as well as the ancient art of dowsing. Forty circles monitored by the team were found to have numerous anomalies of natural background energies, especially in magnetic field strength, infra-red light, ultrasonic noises and Earth energies. Some Stone Circles were found to be shielding out high background radioactivity in granite areas, where levels can be high.

When dawn light hits the Rollright Stones, they were found to discharge high pitched sounds and infra-red outbursts. Infra-red photos of the King Stone have shown a faint auric haze glowing around it at dawn.

From their years of studying Stone Circles, results have led team member Don Robins to surmise that the stones act as condensers, where an electrical charge is stored until something happens, such as when people touch them, at which point the energy is quickly discharged. Many people have reported mild shocks when first touching the stones.

The project concluded that megaliths can emit or alter strong radiations. Stones tested were all found to be located directly over, or very near, geological fault lines. The discovery of these fault lines was made possible by the ancient art of dowsing.

Art of Dowsing

Dowsing is the art of seeking with the subtlest of our senses. It's most common application is in locating underground water supplies, hence it is often called water divining. But there are also limitless applications of this art, from finding lost people to divining health and disease. From ancient origins, today there are many thriving societies of dowsers in the world and it is generally well accepted, but not officially!

How can dowsers find water and other energies? Pioneering studies of dowsing were undertaken by Zaboj Harvalik, an American physicist and adviser to the army. Fascinated by the subject, Harvalik devised an experiment in the 1960's where, at random intervals, differing levels of electric current were passed through the ground. After hundreds of hours of testing his friends and colleagues, he determined that 80% of his subjects could dowse the live current down to just above two milliamperes strength. A smaller group could detect current down to a mere half a milliampere!

Below: A 16th century German dowser.

The magnetic sense, Harvalik found, was as variable as any other of the senses across the population. Amazingly sensitive, German master dowser Wilhelm de Boer, during repeated tests, was able to unfailingly sense a magnetic field produced by an electric current in the ground of just one microampere (one thousandth of one milliampere). De Boer turned out to be far more sensitive than the magnetometer that Harvalik had been using.

In 1968 Harvalik presented his findings at a lecture to other scientists and described human beings as *"living magnetometers of incredible sensitivity... Magnetometric measurements indicate that a dowser reacts to magnetic gradient changes as weak as one millimicrogauss or, expressed another way, 0.00000001 gauss."* Such weak magnetic anomalies can be found everywhere in the Earth's magnetic field – caused by fault lines, cavities, tree roots and also underground water streams, that water diviners find as energy flow zones.

The mechanism of magnetic reception in people and animals became even clearer around 1980, with the discovery of receptors in the form of microscopic magnetite clusters, found at the base of the beak of pigeons. These sensors were later found across the animal kingdom, helping to explain their extraordinary ability for homing and migration.

In people, it is the ridges of the brow that have the greatest concentration of these energy receptors, which are also found down the spine and in muscles to a lesser extent. Instinctive behaviours around finding one's direction and sensing danger are associated with them.

Dowsing is not an individual 'gift', for we are all gifted in its potential. People who take up dowsing gradually develop their inbuilt sensitivity, just as a singer might hone their voice. It's all in the practice!

Megaliths and Water

Water dowsing provides fascinating insights into landscape energetics and the mysteries of the megaliths. Water diviners search for energy emissions arising from underground streams of water that flow through cavities and faultlines. Frenchman M. Louis Merle was the first archeologist to call attention to the phenomena of underground water flows being strongly associated with Sacred Sites. In 1933 he published a book on the subject - *Radiesthesie et Prehistoire*.

Merle described the water patterns that are found continually repeated at sites. Menhirs in France were found to be always located in the fork of two underground streams that are crossed at, or near, their intersection by a third stream. If the megalith has a smooth face, then this will always face the junction. If three streams are found to cross at the same point then a stone above that crossing will always stand vertical. But if the third stream is crossed between the junction of the two other streams and the stone, the stones always lean away from the junction. If the third stream crosses beyond the junction, then the stone would always be leaning towards the junction, it was found.

At Carnac, Merle described the 11 stone rows as being set between roughly parallel underground streams, with any branching or stream inter-connections indicated by stones larger than the others. A second French book on the subject, by Chas Diot, confirmed his findings. And over in England in 1935 Captain Boothy independently made similar dowsing discoveries. For instance, all the ancient boundary marking stones he dowsed were found to be related to underground water.

English dowser and author Guy Underwood went on to find, by dowsing, that Stone Rows and avenues are *"all aligned on systems of parallel fissures"*, the stones positioned between the fissures. The water energies change in polarity according to the two halves of the lunar cycle, the waxing and waning of the moon, he discovered.

Scottish dowser David Cowan writes of finding vertical sinuous waves emitted from Menhirs, that run in *"regimented parallel streams"* and that these have been described as *"invisible magnetic curtains"*. The vertical component of the emission fields arising from water lines can be easily dowsed. As a source of geopathic stress, water energies can affect health even when people live high up in apartments. No-one knows just how high the water energies can rise into the air.

When Underwood studied Menhirs he found them all usually located over important 'blind springs'. This dowseable pattern is called a 'water dome' in America. Dowsers describe the energy phenomena as a vertical shaft of powerfully upwelling water that doesn't break the surface. From this dome, water may exit horizontally in various directions, in flow lines that follow small fractures, giving it a somewhat octopus-like pattern.

In current times Irish dowser Billy Gawn has confirmed the occurrence of blind springs at Sacred Sites previously found by the old dowsers. But he has found them at modern sites too, such as beneath newish gate pillars, under random boulders on hillsides and even under electric pylons!

Some dowsers, such as highly skilled ones in Sweden met by the author, are not convinced that blind springs exist! Others prefer to talk about them as being the intersections of multiple underground streams. Underwood himself noted that it would be *"difficult to imagine how a blind spring could exist and persist in any other rock formation"* [than limestone or chalk].

At Stonehenge, Underwood found the Heel Stone to be located over an important blind spring. He found one precisely in the centre of the circle and one under the altar stone too; while it's Basin Stones he dowsed to be over smaller blind springs.

These days most dowsers would concur that Menhirs are typically located over flows of underground water and especially multiple stream crossings. Billy Gawn finds Stone Circles to have one or more blind springs within the circle, usually in a central location, with several smaller streams flowing away from them. The edge lines of these small streams are also marked with stones, he says.

At Ireland's Turoe Stone (right) the author was surprised to dowse a water line crossing. This would be normal to find at a sacred stone. But after dowsing, it was learnt that the stone had been removed from its former position on a royal hilltop over 150 years ago. Perhaps the person who moved it was a dowser? Or, as a focus of visitor admiration, had the stone itself attracted the water?

Heavy structures, such as big megalithic monuments, affect gravity and underground hydrology. People's consciousness can also affect water energetically. There are tales of Biblical events where springs have gushed forth from the ground as a result of a spiritual act. There are also older traditions of the attraction of water to special sites and especially at megaliths (see the author's book *The Wisdom of Water*). So were the energies and springs at Sacred Sites present first, or did the monuments come first? It's possibly a bit of both.

The proponents of the idea of 'new water' say that water is constantly being created deep inside the Earth, making it's way upwards under pressure and emerging as springs. The theory of new water helps to explain the presence of water at sacred sites generally. Modern megaliths are also known to attract underground water flows to themselves and thus it is wise to consider this possibility when thinking about where to build one's own Stone Circle in a small backyard.

Bio-Electrical Charge

Dowser John Taylor studied a standing stone near Crickhowell in South Wales in 1975 and found around it a significant distortion in the local geomagnetic field. There was a doubling of the normal field strength of half a gauss, so this was quite a variation. The field was found to wax and wane in a regular cycle. Taylor also found narrow bands of double strength geomagnetism running horizontally across the stone at various heights. These were moving up and down in their position somewhat over time, on a seasonal basis, he discovered.

If certain stones are touched, say certain megalithic traditions, one can lose one's memory. More commonly, people experience tingling sensations from touching the stones. A few people even receive mild electrical-like shocks. Effects vary from person to person, with sensitives and dowsers often experiencing shocks the strongest.

When antiquarian and dowser Tom Lethbridge and his wife were trying to dowse the age of the Merry Maidens Stone Circle in Cornwall with their pendulums, they touched them and *"experienced strong electric shocks"*. He went to suppose that bio-electric energy had been imparted and stored in the stones by people dancing in the circle long ago.

Effects vary with the phases of the moon. The strength of reactions is lowest on the sixth day after the new and full moons, at a time when circle energies have been found to reverse polarity. Interestingly – the first day of the month in the old Celtic calendar is six days after the new moon.

Bio-Electrical Charge

Since Taylor's discoveries, other dowsers have mapped out distinct bands of energy that spiral up and down the standing stones. Tom Graves was introduced to the subject during his college days, when he met with engineer Bill Lewis and lawyer John Williams, in Wales. Graves was shown how to sense the energy bands on the standing stones. These, he wrote, were *"energies not just in the movements of the pendulum, but in my fingertips, tingling, like static electricity, like a mild electric shock. Sometimes strong enough to push me to the side, away from the stone"*.

Williams described how, when touching certain Menhirs, a spiralling force built up through the whole body, the person being then thrown to the ground with the force of the energetic discharge.

For a medium to large megalith, Graves found, there will typically be seven energy bands detectable, two of which are below the surface. The 3rd is about at ground level and the rest are above, the 7th being near the top. Smaller stones of up to 150 cm (5 ft) high may have only five bands.

He told of dowsers who experience a particularly strong energy release from a Menhir when, in a sensitive frame of mind, they touch its 5th and 7th energy bands.

"All seven bands, according to several researchers I've talked to, are tapping points into a spiral release of some kind of energy that moves up and down the stone following the lunar cycle ... The spiral feeds energy from the ground to the sky during one half of the lunar cycle and feeds from the sky to the ground during the other half," Graves wrote in *Needles of Stone,* over 30 years ago.

He went on to make the analogy that Standing Stones appear to act as giant acupuncture needles in the Earth. As with human needling, they can provoke a homeostatic (healing, balancing) effect - moving energy in or out, up or down, as required.

Stone Chakras

From where do the Menhir's energy bands originate? Typically located over underground streams of water and particularly where two or more streams cross, or above a blind spring - at such locations dowsers also typically find spiralling vortex energies that may cover the whole site.

Right - The spiral carved stone found inside the Passage Mound of Newgrange in Ireland.

Vortices are not flat. They are multi-dimensional chakra points. Stones placed on Earth chakras can help facilitate the 'breathing' of Earth's energies, bringing homeostasis, and also doubling as portals for inter-dimensional manifestations. Flowing either upwards or downwards, it's a normally downward pulling Earth vortex that is pulled up a Menhir on a water line crossing.

The same effect happens when we deliberately place a Tower of Power on a downward vortex in the garden. It's actually modern day 'megalithic engineering' when we erect these Towers. They can be used to control geopathic stress from water lines, to energise garden plants, as well as enhance the general feng shui of a place.

But are the vortices always flowing downwards? Some dowsers find the opposite at water line crossings, that is, they find upward vortices. And it seems that the vortices may actually come in up/down pairs with the potential to flow both ways at different times or even at once.

A little known phenomena is the presence of a vertical line of smaller vortices running down the central midline of the Menhirs. Curiously human-like, seven of such 'chakra' points may be dowsed along the length of a large megalith and below it. They appear to be points where two spiralling vortex lines cross. These vortices have also been described as a vertical series of connected cones of forces, with alternating polarities.

Stone Chakras can also be found on Power Towers. Where the spiralling energy lines cross at the top are the so-called 'energy doors'. These are points of greatest influence, where energies are flowing in and out most intensely. A Power Tower energy door could well be equivalent to the power points found on the 5th and 7th energy bands associated with the old Menhirs.

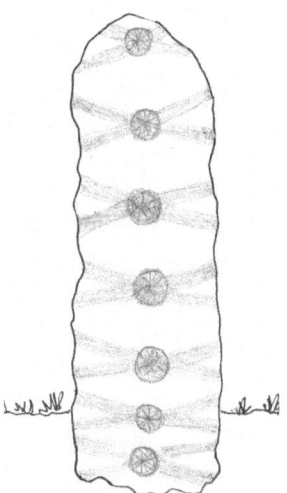

Geodetic Lines

The feng shui masters of old, as well as dowsers of today, detect Earth energy currents that emerge from the ground and flow sinuously across it. These geodetic lines have been likened to serpents and dragons in the past and this comes as no surprise when their snake-like forms are appreciated by dowsing or clairvoyance.

Flowing according to the principles of fluid dynamics, as British dowser scientist Jim Lyons has pointed out, they traditionally enliven the landscape, according to feng shui tradition. The Chinese call them Dragon Lines (*lung mei*).

Menhirs are often found positioned along small geodetic lines. Underwood found that if two or more Boundary Stones are present, that these are not only co-incident with the actual boundary but also with geodetic lines following that boundary.

It was similar with Basin Stones, Underwood found. Not only marked by the presence of blind springs, he also found Basin Stones to have geodetic lines forming a spiral of the same size as the stone. The channel which takes away excess water also marks the place of exit of the geodetic line, he determined.

Some geodetic lines are huge and long. The most well known examples are the Michael and Mary Lines that traverse much of England, running diagonally from the tip of Cornwall up to the coast of East Anglia. Hamish Miller and Paul Broadhurst were the first modern dowsers to trace this mighty dragon line pair as they interwove together, criss-crossing the landscape. They wrote about their discoveries in *The Sun and the Serpent*.

It was found that where these yin and yang currents crossed was typically at important nodes in the landscape, including many Sacred Sites and megalithic monuments. In the Avebury area, for instance, crossing points were found at Windmill Hill, between the two smaller inner circles of Avebury and in the centre of the nearby Sanctuary site. Miller wrote of node points at crossings that exhibited pentagram forms when dowsed with his rods. (The signature shapes changed, at dawn in May 1988, to that of three nested 12 pointed star shapes, one within the other, he reported.)

So are the vortices at fixed points? Dowser John Lamb wrote about finding the Avebury node points to be a moveable feature, in *Dowsing Today* (April 2012). Dowsing at the spring equinox he had found a node located near The Cove, the small northern circle. But returning after the autumn equinox, he dowsed that the node's position had moved over to the south west of the Obelisk Stone, due to, presumably, some sort of seasonal drift.

Leys

Alfred Watkins, a maverick English researcher in the 1920s, made the discovery that ancient sites are often in alignment with one another. He would look down across the hilly Herefordshire landscape from a high spot and see monuments and natural landscape features lining up together. Alignment markers ranged from ancient barrow mounds to modern churches that were often built over ancient sites. Mysterious boulders dotted around the landscape were interpreted by Watkins as marking some of these physical alignments across the land. He was the first to call these alignments 'leys'. They were always straight. Perhaps they provided sight lines for cosmic observations?

Later dowsers came along who went on to discover energetic pathways that co-incided with these alignments, both on the ground and up in the air. These days, official Dowsing Society terminology calls the aerial energy pathways Energy Leys, to distinguish them from physical alignments and geodetic lines.

The Energy Ley system is an aerial network of linear, yang energy lines, somewhat like a spiders web spread across the land. Sometimes pillars of energy connect down from above, linking Energy Leys to megalithic monuments and Sacred Sites on the ground.

Ley marker stones may be found located at nodes or junction points of two or more Energy Leys. The Mark Stones that are touched by this yang energy are themselves touched by people who visit them to charge up their own energies.

Dolmen Energies

Carrowmore megalithic complex in County Sligo, western Ireland, is the largest and most important megalithic centre outside Carnac in France. It dates back to between 3,500 BCE to 500 BCE in parts. Here, across one square kilometre (.38 ml^2), are found some 30 passage mounds in various states of ruin (and there may have once been 200 or more). Once hidden beneath earthen mounds, many have been quarried and are now purely skeletal, with only scraggly Stone Circles and a central Dolmen (looking like a massive stone table) remaining.

It's said that there is an alignment between Carrowmore and Tara in Ireland, which continues on to Stonehenge and the Great Pyramid in

Egypt. While it looks good on a two dimensional map, it's a bit different when it comes to an actually spherical planet, however!

Dowser author Michael Poynder was fascinated by the energies of Carrowmore's Dolmen stones and found them to be located over underground streams. This tallied with the findings of the Heritage Awareness Group in Dublin (now absorbed into the Druid School). When they did dowsing surveys of Newgrange and other sites, the group had found them *"all aligned over crossing points of undergrounds streams,"* Keiran Comerford was informed.

Poynder, who passed away in 2011, also found what he called 'water spirals' that rise upwards at the centre of a Dolmen, where the crossing points of underground streams are found. Billy Gawn describes how he clairvoyantly sees a column of energy, a vortex rising vertically up above the centre of a Dolmen (as well as at Stone Circles). The energy

*Trevethy Quoit
- a Dolmen
near Liskeard
in Cornwall.*

actually flows two ways, he observes – up and down. Earth energy lines that he has observed tend to obey the laws of fluid dynamics (as do clouds), he notes, concuring with scientific thought.

The author's dowsing of the Dolmens at Carrowmore confirmed the central spiral vortices and also that these energetic forms are homes to powerful guardian spirits. The Earth elemental beings are detectable by dowsing for their typically spherical fields of energy.

Sadly, many of the Carrowmore Dolmen are being 'restored' in totally unsympathetic ways, their 'restorers' seemingly only concerned with the eventual visual effect for tourists. Filling the insides with energy-disrupting concrete and steel, their integrity is being destroyed on the pretext of heritage conservation! Such is the insensitive state of Irish archeology these days.

Stone Circle Energies

As well as water lines and domes, Stone Circles are found by dowsers to be associated with various energetic anomalies and patterns, including geodetic flows, vortices, ley nodes, alignments and sacred geometric forms.

Spiralling energies are a common feature of Stone Circles generally, dowsers find. Tom Graves wrote about dowsing a two dimensional concentric circle pattern within the Rollright Stones circle with a group of dowsers in the 1970s. Some felt it might be a spiral. A later researcher, retired BBC engineer Charles Brooker, described the magnetism found inside the Rollright Circle as forming a seven ring spiral that broadened as it flowed outwards via the eastern gate, as reported in *New Scientist* (January 1983). Brooker also described converging leys at the site, as well as two Menhirs that emitted strong magnetic pulses there.

Jim Lyons, the British dowser scientist, has written of the spiderweb matrix pattern commonly found by dowsers at landscape 'Earth acupuncture points', such as Stone Circles. Ring patterns are ubiquitous and these are embedded with radial lines, like a wheel, he says. The commonest number being six rings with eight radial lines. Superimposed over this pattern is a spherical field, the lower half of which is under the ground.

Lyons reports spiderweb energy patterns in association with blind springs and crop circles too, and also in the presence of chalk underlying the surface. Dowsing at Power Towers can also display this spiderweb pattern.

Above: A clairvoyant Polish artist has captured several energetic effects at an old Polish stone circle in the painting above, depicting white, pink and yellow lines of radiant energy flows that emanate from the stones.

A most energetic Stone Circle to dowse is the Swan Circle near Glastonbury, seen on the next page. Despite being only a few years old, it has energetic patterns that one would expect to find at an ancient

circle. It was all the more lively for being complete and intact, unlike those many sad old sites that have been partially destroyed. And being annually frolicked in at the Glastonbury Festival, it is a happy place.

What sort of effects do the sacred stone energies have on people? Researcher Maxwell Cade developed an improved electro-encephalograph for measuring brain waves, in his ground breaking study of altered states of consciousness. He found mind altering affects on people at certain megaliths.

Over several visits to the Rollright Stones he found that people who were tested in the vicinity of some of the Menhirs tended to slip easily into the deep and slow theta and delta brainwave rhythms. In such a mind state one's awareness would be piqued, the veil to other-dimensional worlds might be lifted, powers of self-healing or creative potential accessed. No wonder such sites are rich with tales of resident other-worldly beings and the getting of divine inspiration!

Bora Grounds in Australia

In eastern Australia an Aboriginal equivalent to the British henges are the circular dance sites generally known as Bora Grounds or, in Queensland, Kiparra Rings. These low circular rings are made of either stones or earthen mounds (and sometimes marked by logs), which enclose a flat, smooth area that is kept clear for public dancing, theatre and musical events ('corroborees'). Not just for social events and entertainment, the Boras were also associated with initiation ceremonies. Examples include Boras in the form of circles of individually arranged stones located in Werrikimbe National Park in northern New South Wales.

Typically a larger Bora Ring is paired with a smaller one. Larger rings were for general, public corroborees and they were linked by a sacred way marked on the ground, sometimes enclosed within earthen banks, that lead on to the smaller, sacred initiation grounds. In one report boys would walk along this connecting path, representing the transition from childhood to manhood, and stop where there were stone arrangements or bark or timber effigies, the points where tribal wisdom was passed on to them. Sometimes the initiates followed footsteps (mundoes) cut into rock pavements. The boys would start the ceremony in the larger, public ring, and end it in the other, smaller, one, to which only they and the initiated men were admitted. Sadly, in the handful of preserved examples visited by the author, the smaller second ring has typically been lost.

In the centre of some large Bora Grounds are found depressions that were used as fire places. In others, mounds of rocks or decorated tree trunks feature in the centre.

John Currie described ceremonies held at the Tucki Tucki Bora Ground in northern New South Wales around 1875. A huge fire would burn in the centre of the main Bora Ground, which is about 20 m (66 ft) in diameter. Men and women, painted vividly with white clay stripes, would sit on opposite sides of the ring, all singing together, or watching various performers sing and dance. The track to the smaller circle was some 100 m (110 yd) long. Today only 14 m (46 ft) remains and the rest of it plus the smaller ring are lost in a farmers field.

In the centre of the smaller initiation ring Currie observed a large upturned tree stump, its roots fanning outwards and brightly decorated with red vines stripped of their bark to show their colour. (This echoes global symbolism of the central, sacred World Tree omphalos, a subject which will be returned to when looking at Labyrinths.) An old man sat on top of this tree and spoke to the young boy initiates, occasionally throwing sacred pebbles to the ground. The tree may well have been used as a physical prop by tribal 'clever men', a launching pad for shamanic journeying into other worlds to commune with the spirits.

Not surprisingly, the Bora Grounds are found, by dowsing, to be pulsing with powerful energies. Dowsing typically finds an upward energy vortex in the larger of the rings, being an emerging geodetic line that one might call a Serpent Line. This then flows along the connecting pathway and, at the centre of the other, smaller ring, it exits via a downward vortex.

At the biennial Laura Dance Festival that was held over a weekend in June 2011 in Cape York Peninsula, far north Queensland, the author witnessed around 500 Aboriginal people dancing on an ancestral Bora Ground. The Earth Spiral vortex dowsed on that dusty circular site grew and grew in intensity over the days.

By Monday morning, as the festival was packing up, the pendulum recorded an extraordinary amount of energy pouring upwards out of the Earth. It was the most powerful Earth Spiral I had ever dowsed!

Landscape Temples

The spiderweb pattern found at individual Sacred Sites has a larger manifestation of an etheric web of connections across the land. Ritual sites are found to be linked together in networks of geometric alignments with other sites, as well as by geodetic lines and aerial energy leys. Regionally such a grouping of sites might be called a Landscape Temple. Just as with ecological connections in nature, sites thus connected may feel any damage done to one of their 'kin', however distant, with others in the surrounding web potentially mal-affected.

Where might you start to look for a regional Landscape Temple? Check out your local geographical zones and boundaries. Water is a common feature of many Sacred Sites, so hydrological patterns will often determine site positions and connections. A Landscape Temple could well be found contained within your local watershed - the water catchment area. In permaculture we call it the Bio-Region.

Old tribal boundaries and maps can also be a guide to the location of Sacred Sites. For example, in southern Tasmania the hot springs at Hastings is a Sacred Site for all the adjacent tribes and it was used for inter-tribal gatherings, the various clan territories all converging there.

Avebury is one of the best known of the European Landscape Temples. It is an impressive complex spread over several miles and it includes not just the great Stone Circle and its avenues, but also the Sacred Sites of Windmill Hill, Silbury Hill and West Kennett Barrow. On its hilltops beacons were once lit in the area to signal the May Day sunrise.

In the 17th century Stukely saw Avebury in a more complete light. A great many more stones existed then, though they were being removed and destroyed at a fast rate. He sensed it's original purpose and drew it thus (- his visionary plan is on the next page). The Sanctuary, or Hackpen, represented a huge serpents head; indeed, the whole complex was a *"centre for serpent worship"*, he felt. The serpent has long been symbolic of Earth's lifeforce and wisdom, so he was probably correct!

Landscape Temples

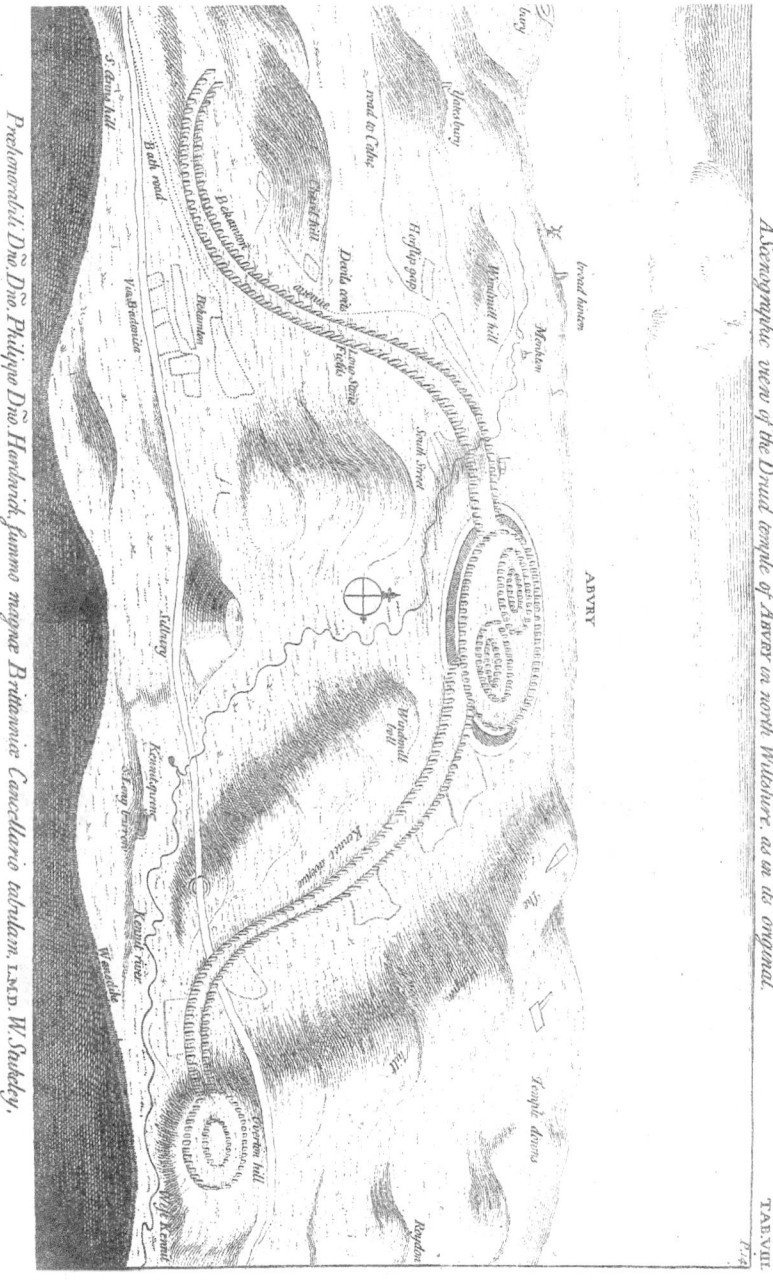

67

Certainly, Avebury was part of a ritual landscape of sites used for ceremony and pilgrimage. As for the famous Henge, Hamish Miller mused that *"the raw energy of the Earth was the serpent fertilised by the opposing cosmic forces of the Sun and Moon, concentrated in the great circle, the generative organ of the whole complex."*

In Australian Aboriginal geomancy, landscapes marked with significant features such as rocks, hilltops, caves and the like are considered to provide evidence for mythic journeys of huge ancestral snakes and other totemic spirits during the creative Dreamtime. Songlines, the musical stories that record these journeys and connect the landscape features together, often head off into the sky to connect with the stars. Aboriginal lore has its echoes in the sacred landscapes of Avebury. Such enduring legacies have global currency. We are most fortunate to inherit some of the sacred Touchstones that point us back towards a magical connection to Mother Earth.

Above: Dingo Dog Rock, one of many sacred geomythic stones around Alice Springs, in central Australia.
Right: This dragon rock is one of many special stones that feature in the beautiful Chinese Gardens in Darling Harbour, Sydney, Australia, where good feng shui rules!

Landscape Temples

Chapter 3: Megaliths and Petroglyphs

Central Australian Aboriginal petroglyphs at Ewaninga, south of Alice Springs.

'Art' of the Petroglyphs

Across the vast continent of Australia, the most numerous Aboriginal rock 'art' motifs are cupules (also known as cup marks), circles and arcs. These forms are the oldest types of petroglyphs known, with a pair of arcs dated to around 40,000 years of age. Other common shapes are animal tracks and abraded grooves.

Globally, petroglyphs can be found carved on natural rock outcrops and boulders, as well as on megalithic stone arrangements. Also found worldwide, cupules are cup shaped depressions, also called pits, dots or hollows.

Cupules in an overhang at Mutawintji National Park, in far south west New South Wales

In Australia they are typically about 5 cm (2 in) diameter and 3cm (1 in) deep, often found in large groups, sometimes on steep or vertical rock surfaces, and typically featuring at Sacred Sites. In one example, a spectacular rock shelter in the Kimberleys has thousands of cupules covering the vertical walls and sloping ceiling.

Aboriginal society had no word or concept for 'art'. The act of making petroglyphs was more ritual working than artistic expression. The underlying belief was that the act of marking rock by hammering or rubbing (resulting in hollows and abraded grooves) can produce wish fulfillment. This is why they are typically found at Sacred Sites, where ceremonies for increase and maintenance of Country were performed.

Totemic spirits reside permanently at Sacred Sites. Increase rituals performed there invoke the creative powers of these spirits, in order to enhance the fertility of particular plant or animal species. In Europe some of the cupules came to be explained as the marks of dancing fairies, with offerings of flowers and fruits once made to them there.

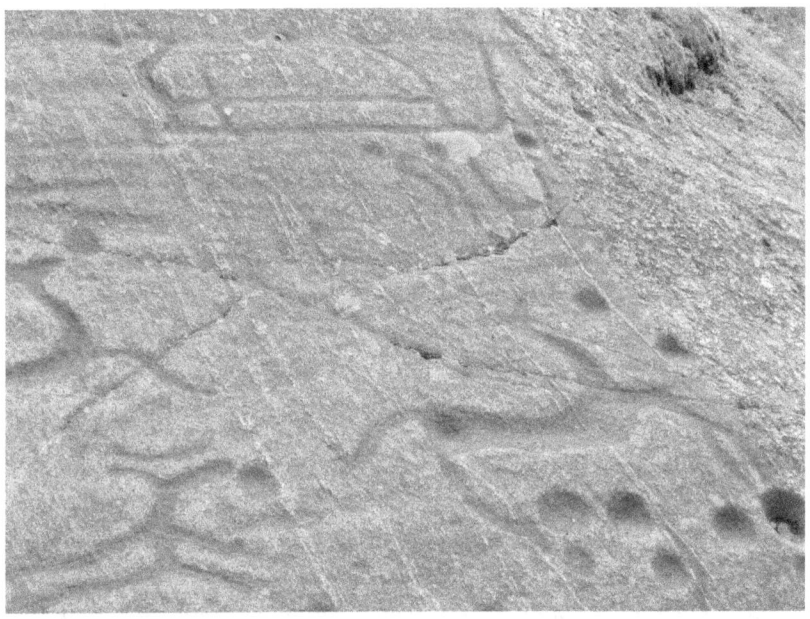

Above: Ships, deer and cupules adorn a Swedish petroglyph site (also page 81).

The abraded groove type of petroglyph is typically a series of straight line rubbing marks. These are known to have been created during rain making rituals.

And animal tracks in stone are thought to have been made for improving luck with hunting.

Thus rather than being 'art', ancient petroglyphs are more likely the by-products of symbolic action.

America's Ringing Rocks

Paul Deveraux takes an even more kinetic approach to unravelling the mystery of the cupules. In his book *Stone Age Soundtracks*, he writes of Ringing Rocks, natural stones at certain Sacred Sites, often covered with cupules, that when struck percussively would make bell or drum like sounds.

The repeated striking of the rock with a hammerstone, to create the cupule, would have made an other-wordly music, as well as echoes that may have been interpreted as the devas calling back.

Deveraux also notes that *"rock art expert Jack Steinberger has proposed that making cupules and grooves involves rhythmic sounds and action, that itself can be trance inducing."*

Of Bell Rock in Orange County California (now in the Bowers Museum in Santa Ana), Deveraux describes this best known of America's Ringing Rocks as a seven tonne boulder with numerous cupules. He tells us, from an old account, that *"around this boulder native Indians gathered in ancient times. With stone mortars they pounded upon it and the canyon rang with the clear tones of this primitve bell."*

Another such Ringing Rock, in Tulare County, is also covered in cupules. Passing Yakut Indians would stop there and *"ring the bells"*, striking the rocks before continuing their journeys.

At a third example, in Saskatchewan, Canada, the Herschel Petroglyph site is associated with bison hunting. At the base of a monolithic rock, below where bison were once herded off a cliff, the rock is covered with hundreds of cupules, and bone offerings were also buried there. It is suggested that the sound of many cupules being pounded together would have mimicked the thundering sounds of herds of galloping bison.

Australian Aboriginal Ritual

Australian Aboriginal culture is the oldest continuing culture in the world and there is much to be learnt from it. Charles Mountford is believed to be the first to record the production and function of pounded cupules by Aboriginal people in Australia. In the 1940's Mountford observed cupules being created by Aboriginal men in the traditional manner in the Musgrave Ranges, south east of Uluru, central Australia.

Mountford described the curiously shaped boulder there that was said to be the body of Pink Cockatoo Woman Tukalili. (The cockatoo was, at that time, an important food source in the region.) The men pounded the Tukalili boulder with small hammerstones during an increase ceremony.

He was told that this action *"causes the release of the kuranita (life essence) of the cockatoo, with which the boulder is impregnated. This kuranita, rising into the air in the form of dust, fertilises the living female cockatoos, causing them to lay more eggs."*

Mountford later recorded numerous other such ceremonies that included the rubbing of rock surfaces for the purpose of increase and to ritually enfuse the spirit of place into the greater landscape.

Cosmological Petroglyphs

Abraded grooves may also have served calendrical functions, says Hugh Cairns, who, together with Wardaman elder Bill Yidumduma Harney, wrote the very first book on Aboriginal cosmology. Cairns believes that he has discovered patterns of grooves which suggest a marking of time by moon phases.

Cairns was first alerted to possible astronomical explanations for some petroglyphs in the 1970's, when he and expert guide John Lough went viewing some of the thousands found scattered across the rugged sandstone escarpments of the Kuringai National Park area, north of Sydney. A group of engraved cupules seen by Cairns there matched *"almost exactly the Orion and Scorpius patterns"* and it spurred him on to further research into Aboriginal cosmology. In 1979 he found the Star Stone, which has a Scorpius pattern of cupules. It points the direction towards where that constellation is seen mid-year. And nearby, the Calendar Stone has two series of cupules that seem to match moon phases, next to a pattern resembling Hyades, he says.

Remnants of the local Aboriginal language record several star names. There are words for Pleiades, Orion, Southern Cross, Scorpius and the Magellan clouds. No doubt there were other words too, now lost.

Above: Australian Aboriginal engraving at the Basin Track in Kuringai Chase National Park, near Sydney. Astro-archeologist Ray Norris thinks that it may represent a lunar eclipse, with a Moon-Man obscuring the Sun-Woman (or vice-versa) as an explanation for the event. Crescent shapes are often found in the numerous carvings in the soft sandstone. While they were once thought to represent boomerangs, they are actually not shaped like boomerangs at all, rather, they appear to show the crescent moon.

The night sky has provided navigational maps for indigenous people the world over. Movements of certain stars have provided the timing for human life events too. The Wardaman have their sky Song Lines - epic story paths that criss-cross the night sky, connecting Earth and cosmos, and providing the timing for preparation for ceremonies. There are a host of powerful spirit beings in the Wardaman sky lore and their adventures are played out each year in the progress of the Song Lines.

An outstanding Song Line emanates from the Pleiades, Cairns was informed. It joins another from Leo, home of the Creation Dog (a dingo spirit) and begins in April. It then travels onwards to the Southern Cross. The Pleiades line is that through which young people's education and initiation is planned, in the lead-up to October ceremonies, before the Wet season arrives. Similar stories associated with the stars are told around the rest of Australia too.

Cairns found other cupules and markings that suggest star patterns and moon phases at Mutawintje and nearby Panaramittee, in far south west New South Wales. In Western Australia, Cairns saw evidence of astronomical observation, including a site where rock engravings *"include one matching the pattern of Crux. It is within one metre of a pillar, a placed stone that acts as a back sight. It's shape fits exactly an undisputedly grooved front-sight. If you line them up this fixes the west direction, that is moonset/sunset,"* he wrote.

Some petroglyphs in India also display astronomical patterns. A square table-like rock with a slanting top, examined by a team from the University of Hyderabad, shows cupules from the megalithic era in a pattern said to be the Great Bear constellation, also known as Ursa Major and Saptarshi Mandala in India. It could well be the earliest depiction of a star map in the country, they reported in April 2006.

The pattern of cupules shows a rectangle and a tail-like formation of three cups/stars. This star pattern has long been used by travellers and sea voyagers as pointers to the pole star to identify exact north. (The Great Bear is also seen in northern Australia, where it is an important constellation to the Wardaman and home to some of their totemic beings.)

The site of the Indian megalith has a *"resemblance to Stonehenge in England"* and is home to other petroglyph star maps. There are some 80 Menhirs standing up to 4.2 m (14ft) tall, while hundreds of smaller ones are scattered over farmland fields at Mudumula village, in the Mahabubnagar district of Andrah Pradesh state.

In Lascaux, amidst the famous cave paintings of central France, are found star patterns painted around 16,500 years ago. Seen close to the entrance is a magnificent painting of a bull and *"hanging over its shoulder is what appears to be a map of the Pleiades, the cluster of stars sometimes called the Seven Sisters"* researcher Dr Rappenglueck, of the University of Munich, reported on BBC News Online (9-8-2000). Rappenglueck thinks the cave paintings at Lascaux (and some in Spain of 14,000 years age) may be the earliest evidence for humanity's interest in the stars.

The Pleiades region is still associated with bulls – it is part of the Taurus/ Bull Constellation. The Pleiades, which leave the northern sky in spring and reappear in the fall, still mark planting and harvesting cycles for many cropping farmers around the world, both in the northern and southern hemispheres.

While cupules have been around for some 30-40,000 years or more in Australia, they may go back to hundreds of thousand of years in Africa, Europe and India, according to researcher Robert Bednarik. North America has its pit-and-groove style of rock 'art', often found as exclusive groups of isolated cupules, and the style is thought to constitute the oldest type of petroglyphs there.

Cup Marks in Britain

In Britain cup-and-ring petroglyphs are fairly numerous between Yorkshire and northern Scotland, although a few are also found in Derbyshire. They are found clustered on stones of all sizes and on rock faces, caves, chambered mounds and souterrains (underground cavities). Some people think that these petroglyphs functioned as symbols of magical protection.

British petroglyphs are often found associated with the boundaries of ancient settlements and common forms are sometimes seen on ceramics too. In areas of large-scale ritual landscapes, petroglyphs have been found to mark the main routes into the ritual area.

Mike Haigh, writing in *Northern Earth* magazine, describes how *"along the principal route to the Milfield Basin in Northumberland it has been found that each major decorated rock is intervisible from the next, so that travellers are led towards this important Henge complex."*

Typically, a British cup mark is a little hollow, either round or sometimes oval shaped, and in size between 12 mm (.5 in) and 15 cm (6 in) diameter. Actual cup-and-ring motifs are much rarer and they may signify a later elaboration on the plain cupule. Rings around the cups typically feature a groove going through them, coming from the cup.

From observations of cup marks with a groove projecting out from a central hollow, dowser Michael Cook has found that *"if one puts a stave in the cup-and-ring mark and lines it up with the line and stands behind the staff and looks along the staff and the line – there will be another site on that line, or a feature on the horizon."*

Dowsing the Petroglyphs

Another researcher, dowser David Cowan in Scotland, has described the cup-and-ring marks of Perthshire in his books. When I visited David in September 2006 he showed me his favourite megalith, a big recumbent stone that sits in a field above a fault line - the Highland Boundary Fault (pictured next page). This is a typical location for all the stones with petroglyphs in the highly faulted Highland country, he said.

"There's a spiral of energy that comes up into this stone," he said, *"and that's where it gets its energy from"*. The stone is covered with some 60 cup and ring marks that have been dated to around 4,000 years of age. By dowsing, Cowan has discovered energy lines that emanate from the stone's petroglyphs and spread out across a wide area, going for miles. The pattern of the petroglyphs appear to him to be a mirror, or virtual map of the energies of the region.

So faint were the cupules that if I hadn't been shown the markings I don't think I would have spotted them.

"Thirty years ago, when I first got interested in the subject, the petroglyphs were very pronounced on this stone. Now they are getting very faint, no doubt from the effects of acid rain," he told me.

Cowan found that if he chisels onto a stone a cup-and-ring mark, with a groove going out from the centre, and then places it, correctly orientated according to dowsing, beside a house that is affected by noxious energies - it truly does have a protective effect!

While the purpose of all of the ancient petroglyphs cannot ever be fully known, they could well be mankind's oldest global expression of connection to the environment and all its dimensions, via ritualised and symbolic interaction with stone.

Dowsing the Petroglyphs

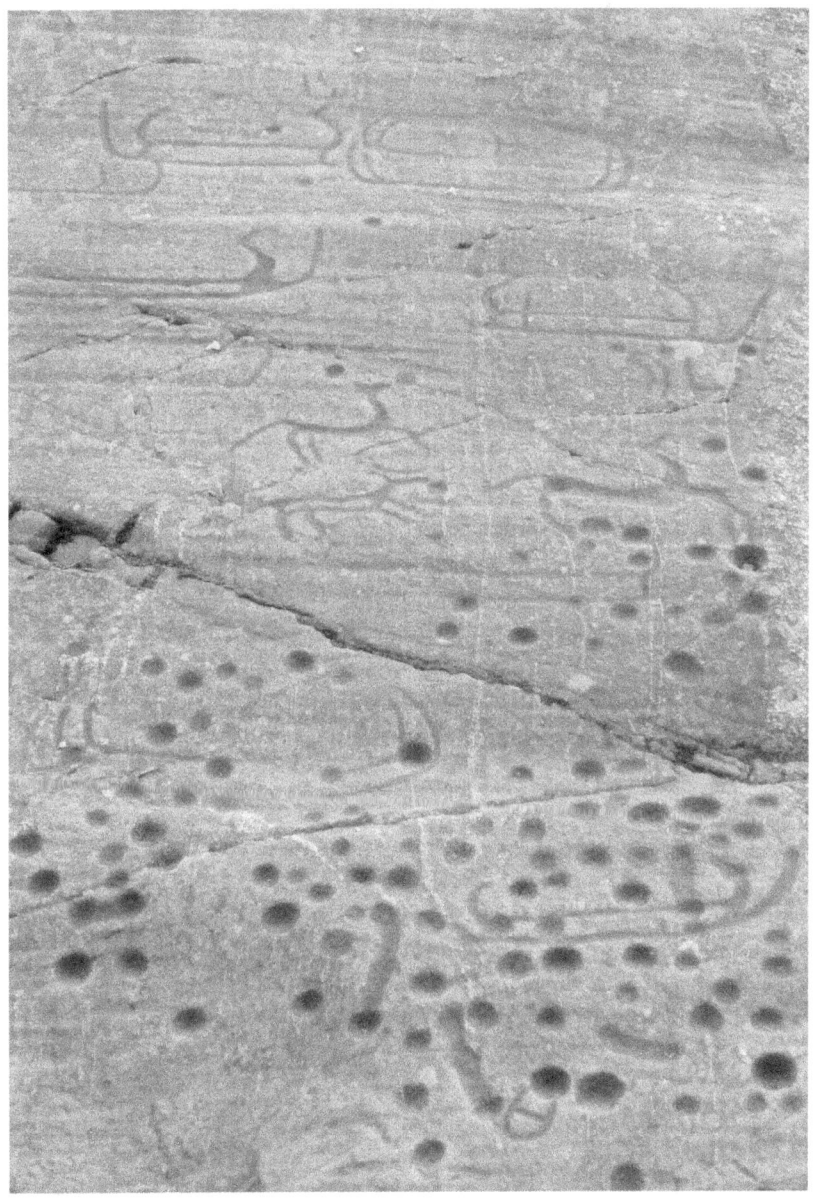

Swedish petroglyphs of boats are said to probably symbolise the voyage to the afterlife of the dead. Boat shaped Stone Circles are found in ancient Swedish burial grounds.

Chapter 4: Creating Stone Arrangements

A modern sculpture by Donato Rosella in a roundabout in Lismore, northern New South Wales, Australia.

Stone Circle Revival

Since the late 1970's the art of Stone Circle building has been enjoying a revival. From Europe to North America and Australia, people are discovering that they love the aesthetic appeal, the sacred expression of environmental art and Earth ritual. They want their circles to be astronomical markers, incorporating various alignments for celestial observation; and as sacred space in which to conduct ceremonies or to connect with the other-dimensional realms. The circle itself has long been symbolic of sacred and protected space.

One of the first full sized Stone Circles to be completed in modern times was back in 1991 at Glen Innes in New South Wales, Australia. Now considered probably the most spectacular of modern circles, its stones rise 3.6 m (12 ft) - 4.5 m (15 ft) above the ground and weigh between 15 - 30 tonnes each. The Circle came about as a community project to honour Australia's Celtic heritage, an idea originating back in 1988, when the Celtic Council of Australia decided to make a national monument to honour all Celtic people who came here. Glen Innes vied to take this on and was selected for the Australian Standing Stones, that were inspired by Scotland's Ring of Brodgar in the Orkneys. With no money for the project, the local council nonetheless took it on wholeheartedly.

The rocky Glen Innes region was scoured for 40 suitable granite monoliths. Most had to be drilled from the bedrock, each stone averaging 17 tonnes in weight. Sponsors were invited to each contribute $1,000 towards costs and within a fortnight all monetary needs had been met. Eventually a circle of 24 stones, one for each hour of the day, was erected. There are also four cardinal stones marking the directions and seven other stones marking the solstices, the longest and shortest days of the year, plus three 'guide stones' that help to mark out the Southern Cross star formation. After a huge amount of volunteer effort, the stones, situated in the Centennial Parklands, were officially opened in February 1992. Each year, on the first weekend in May, they are the venue for an Australian Celtic Festival.

English Druid Ivan Macbeth is regarded as one of the world's experts in Stone Circle building (now based in Vermont, USA). In 1992 Macbeth's first and most famous large Stone Circle, the Swan Circle, was constructed at Worthy Farm, site of the annual Glastonbury Festival in Somerset, UK. To best fit into the site, the 'Circle' is actually egg shaped, with a long axis that aligns with sunrise on the longest day of the year. It also incorporates stones that respresent the Cygnus star group, inspired by the sight of seven swans flying in formation over the field during the planning phase.

In America Rob Roy has been building neo-megalithic Stone Circles since the late 1970's. Visitors marvel at his gate stone – 1.8 m (6 ft) high and weighing in at some 1,360 kg (3,000 lb). Roy, author of a hefty book on the subject, also edits a biennial magazine for Stone Circle builders and keeps a website (bigstones.com). A photo of the Australian Standing Stones features on the cover of Roy's *Stone Circles* book.

Roy prefers to use twelve stones in his large Circles, which, he says, is also the most common number of stones in the British Stone Circles. And he likes to use stones that are really big! But you don't have to always 'think big' to get good results!

Small Circles for the Garden

American natural farmer and author Harvey Lisle was probably the first to discover that small Stone Circles bring benefits to gardens and farms. Lisle places stones in small circles around the trunks of trees, which subsequently enjoy improved growth or healing.

Stone mulching is good to do for many reasons – it helps with moisture retention, remineralisation and temperature regulation for the soil; prevention of soil erosion and damage from pests or pets, etc. But the special energy created when stones are placed deliberately in circles is a bonus! Stone Circles can really enhance the energetic values of a place, with beneficial effects that can be quite far-reaching.

Lisle places his Circles of paramagnetic stones at from 30 cm (1 ft) to 90 cm (3 ft) away from tree trunks. He uses eight double-fist-and-upward sized stones. These are placed in alignment with the four cardinal points, with another stone in between each of them. A Circle of four is enough for a smaller shrub or berry plant, he finds.

"Those Stone Circles around my fruit trees emit low-energy patterns and since I now have more than 100 Stone Circles in my orchard their energy criss-crosses it and is everywhere in the orchard," he wrote. Fruit trees that had been struggling went on to flourish.

Above: In Esperance, Western Australia, they were fortunate to acquire local red granite pieces to make beautiful community garden beds with. The rock is mildly paramagnetic and and the whole garden has a most wonderful vibration!

Making Sacred Circles

For the eco-spiritually minded, stone arrangements can provide wonderful sacred spaces for ritual use. And they can be very simple. It's what goes on within them that is most important!

Before a sacred stone arrangement is made, the site is first carefully selected, by dowsing or meditational attunement. A site with powerful and harmonious energies could well be perfect for a sacred Circle, but always establish if permission may be had from the spirits of the land before going ahead. If the Circle has astronomical functions, make sure the site has good visibility to the horizon and that it will not become blocked out.

Begin by discovering (dowsing is easiest) where the central point of the Circle is best located. This may well turn out to be an Earth vortex, which can function as an energy portal. Standing on that spot with feet bare, go into a meditative state of mind, whereby your sensitivity is piqued. Introduce yourself to the place, either out loud or silently. You might also place a little offering there, such as a flower or pebble. Visualise what you are planning to do there. Ask the spirits of place if your Circle plan is acceptable to them. Wait for a response. When permission is granted, thank and honour the place or its beings.

The site can then be purified and blessed, using techniques such as visualisation, singing, smudging with incense, using crystal wands, harmonic sounds or chanting. For American Circle builder Selena Fox this purification begins at the centre and spirals out around the site.

To make an outdoor sacred Circle, which can be of any diameter, gather your stones, having first gained permission from the stones themselves before acquiring them! It's a good idea to match the size of the stones to the site selected. Determine whether you wish to have a stone for a central altar, or as a meditation seat, or a fire in the centre, or nothing at all. (Ancient British Stone Circles rarely have a central altar stone.)

An easy method to make a Stone Circle is summarised as follows.

* Find the Circle's central point (ideally, but not essential - an appropriate Earth Chakra) and prepare the site by clearing it physically and psychically.

* Drive a temporary wooden peg in at this centre.

* Attach a rope that is the length of the required radius of the Circle. Stretch the rope out fully, then walk with it around the centre, checking with a compass for the location of the cardinal points. (True North needs to be adjusted from the magnetic north.)

* At each of the four quarters place your four best or largest stones. Construction is traditionally made in sunwise order, that is - clockwise in the northern hemisphere and anti-clockwise in the south. Orient or align each stone in the Circle by aesthetic consideration or by dowsing. What looks or feels right, probably is right!

* You might wish to just make a simple four stone Circle, otherwise, for an eight stone ring, place a stone equidistant between each of the four cardinal stones. Or two stones equidistant between the four, for a twelve stone ring. Or three stones in between for a sixteen stone circle.

* You may wish to place a larger or most special stone in the central position, after removing the wooden peg. This might be positioned as a seat for sitting meditation.

* Dowse for an entry / exit point for the circle and always use it! Make this spot obvious, such as by placing a couple of extra rocks there.

* By methodical dowsing at all stages of its construction, you will more easily gain the required altered states of consciousness for good ritual stone arranging work.

* Bless and dedicate the Stone Circle, ready for use. (More on this aspect starts on page 126.)

Mini Stone Circles

"There's no limit to the size of stones that can be used. A Stone Circle can be made from big stones or tiny pebbles", says Ken Ring. Others are in agreement and thus anyone can experience the energies of a Stone Circle first hand, whether it is out in the garden, or in the form of pebbles arranged on a table in your home.

What sort of stones are suitable? Any can be used. Smooth water washed pebbles are a good choice. Check what the local quarry has to offer. And always ask the stones first, such as by dowsing, if they want to work with you!

If you have room for a pair of Circles, you might like them to be dynamic opposites. One could be made of paramagnetic basalt rock, vermiculite or red granite; and a second one of quartz (like the one in the photo above) or white granite, which is diamagnetic. (Paramagnetic stones having a weak attraction to a magnet, diamagnetic stones are weakly repulsed.) Thus you will have a yang and a yin Stone Circle with complementary energies. It's interesting to feel their different subtle effects when ritually walking the Circles. Yang energy being generally stimulating and yin energy having a more calming effect.

On an even smaller scale, a circular plate or tray of sand can make a perfect base for a mini Stone Circle. Dowse to find the best energy spot to position it. Otherwise anywhere will do. Using a compass to find the four directions, you can lay out an eight or twelve pebble Circle. Place four stones, your largest or most prominent ones, at the cardinal points and then one or two inbetween them.

Now to play! You might try dowsing for a spherical energy field that is generated by the Circle. Discover how far it radiates out in all directions. Ask, by dowsing, to find where an entrance / exit point might be. Use an index finger, or palm of the hand to do your Stone Circle 'walking'. Start energy scanning from the entrance point, then trace your finger/hand slowly around the circle a few times, just above the stones.

You might experience the energy as a buzz or tingle in your finger or  the palm as it traces around the Circle. You may feel an energetic difference at the Circle entrance, or between a quartz Circle and a basalt one. You might also find you can attain an altered state of consciousness more easily from this activity and that your meditation could become enhanced.

If you are interested in astronomy you can use your Circle to relate your position to that of the celestial bodies above. A good book to explain more on this aspect, and geared for the southern hemisphere, is by New Zealand's Ken Ring, who is fascinated with the ancient British Stone Circles and uses his knowledge of Moon cycles to predict weather.

As for the healing potential - a sick plant will enjoy being encircled by stones for a few days and may well regain its health. You may feel improved wellbeing from sitting within a tiny Stone Circle at regular intervals yourself. A glass of water can be energised by being placed for a while within your circle too. Experiment!

Garden Miniliths

At the start of planting in springtime, traditional South American farmers brought out the sacred carved stones that represent Earth Mother Pachamamma and placed them in their fields, so that She could watch beneficiently over the crops.

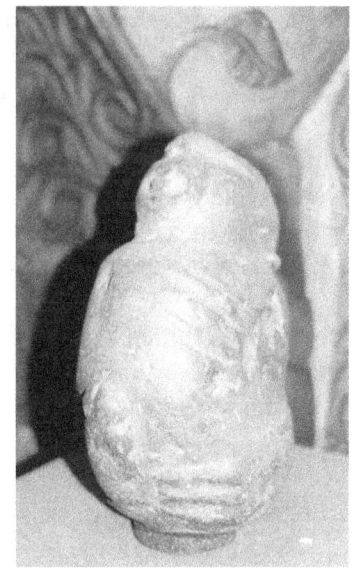

Likewise in New Zealand, carved 'God Stones', such as the museum piece on the right, were once ceremoniously placed in the fields before spring planting of the Maori's crops, especially the sweet potato. Rongo, God of Agriculture, could then use it as His seat, watching and protecting the crops over the growing season.

Rongo has big eyes for this and His stone body is shaped just like the fat kumara tubers that were wished for. His association with virility is also obvious. South America is where the sweet potato hails from, thus the tradition spread out from there across the vast Polynesian region along with the crop several thousands of years ago.

The quartz crystal craze that swept Australia in the 1980s switched many people on to the inherent powers in stones. Many of those crystals were placed in garden beds, with very good results of plant growth enhancement. But what people didn't realise is that interesting energetic effects can be produced by careful placements of small, fairly ordinary looking rocks. Such rocks don't need to be mined from out of the ground, as is done in Brazil, where many crystals are sourced from.

In the early 1980s Gerald Makin of Tasmania, was getting nowhere with his gardening. But when he discovered dowsing he read with great interest about ancient megalith cultures. Dowsing indicated to Makin that it would be possible to enhance soil fertility by placing a standing stone in his garden. By dowsing he determined that a stone he had would fit the bill. He dowsed a position for the stone distantly on a garden plan, as well as its depth and orientation, and then set it up.

As a result of this stone placement Makin subsequently detected a geodetic energy line going from his stone to a neighbouring garden, where an elderly Cornish woman friend also had a Standing Stone. (She was versed in ancient and secret Cornish mystery tradition of geomancy, cosmology and magic.)

Things didn't start really moving, however, until several other stones were erected and energy lines criss-crossed the .5 acre (2,000 m^2) garden. By then the original stone was radiating about 30 energy lines, while an energy spiral that had formed around it filled the whole garden.

Beside each garden bed he placed a small stone, over 30 in all, to carry and transmit Earth energies. From then on, Makin's garden began to flourish as never before!

More recently dowsers have found similar energetic results from using isolated minilithic stones. In 2012 dowser Linda Prenter wrote of dowsing the energies around a small stone arrangement in a British garden. It was a lingam and yoni pair of stones from India (similar to the lingams pictured next page). The lingam, weighing some 2.5 tonnes and rising to 1.5 m (5 ft) in height, represents the phallus of god Shiva;

Garden Miniliths

together with the yoni, they are the inseparable yang and yin of creation. So one would expect some stimulating energies to be present!

Indeed, Prenter found 12 spiral energy lines swirling around it, shaped like a clockspring, flowing anticlockwise in and clockwise out from the south side of the stones. Four straightish radial lines of energy crossed at the stones. It was that old spiderweb pattern again! As the owners were not dowsers one can assume that these energies had been produced as a result of the stones being put there in the recent past.

The Power Towers that were inspired by Irish Round Towers seem to fill the place of the Menhirs of old. They are dowsed as having the same types of dowseable energy patterns as the Menhirs, being also located over water line crossings.

Usually made from crushed volcanic basalt rock that is poured into a pipe or equivalent, they can also be made from stacked red bricks (as on the right) and upside down terracotta pots.

Making Medicine Wheels

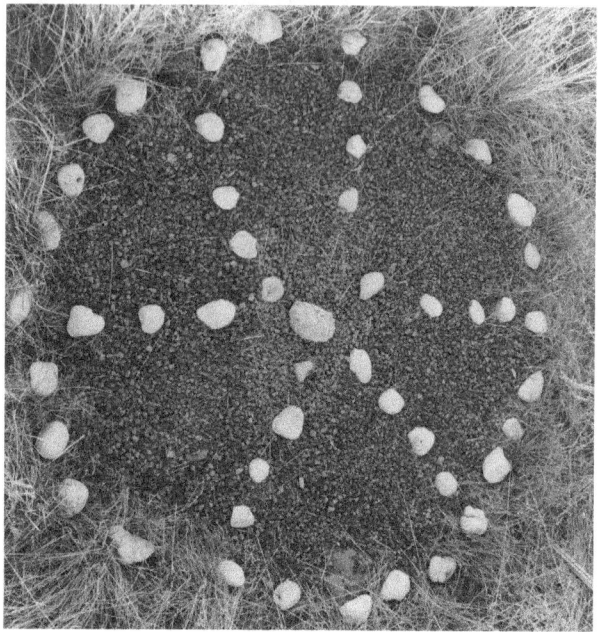

To make a simple Medicine Wheel, such as the one above, you might experiment with a minimum of 12 stones plus a central one, or dowse the number, or use any number. Follow the general approach to sacred Stone Circle making.

* Dowse for a high energy point to locate it and peg the centre.

* Work out the number of stones needed.

* Make a circle of stones around the centre, using a rope on the peg.

* Divine for the number and location of the spokes of the wheel.

* Mark the spokes with lines of smaller stones.

* Bless and dedicate your new Medicine Wheel.

Harvey Lisle has been a pioneering researcher into the modern uses of such Medicine Wheels. *"On my farm,"* he said *"I have east-west and north-south ley lines, which are to the Earth as nerves are to us. Where these two ley lines intersect I have established my Medicine Wheel.*

"From this Medicine Wheel I can control a number of functions on my farm. I think everyone who loves his land has a very special spot on his land and this is the spot to establish your Medicine Wheel," wrote Lisle, in 1988. (His ley lines being, presumably, those aerial energy flows that are today called Energy Leys.)

Canadian dowser Henry Dorst has gained other fascinating insights. His dowsing observations of environmental energy lines at Medicine Wheels both old and new are revealing.

"After inspecting one Medicine Wheel in Alberta and finding two ley lines converging on its centre I assumed that the native builders of such monuments chose them because they had somehow dowsed these energies. I was disavowed of this notion after building a brand-new wheel, and again, after helping construct two Labyrinths.

"In all of these cases - brand-new, dowseable water domes and ley lines appeared after people began to use these constructions meditatively. In other words, my assumption that aboriginal North Americans necessarily dowsed – in the way that we understand dowsing – for these energy phenomena before setting up a site for sacred practices, was erroneous," he wrote.

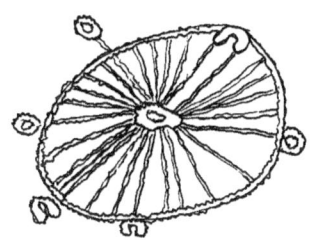

Chapter 5: Labyrinths

Labyrinth Lore

Labyrinths, Turf Mazes and Troy Towns are ancient mandala-like patterns that are found globally. Usually formed with stones, they were also made with mounded earth, hedge plants and turf. Forms include spirals, crosses and swastikas, and there are square and round forms too. Some, as in South America, are huge labyrinthine animal shapes, like gigantic creatures spread across the barren Nasca desert region.

A Labyrinth is not the same as a maze. A Labyrinth has only one path and no dead ends. Unicursal, the way in is also the way out. You can't become lost. The path leads you circuitously to the center and out again.

Labyrinths have an ancient lineage. One of the oldest known, from 5,000 B.C.E. in Mesopotamia, was created to honor the Great Goddess Inanna. This Classic Labyrinth has seven circuits that lead into the center. In the old myths, the Goddess Inanna had to give up a part of Her identity as She descended down through seven levels of the Underworld. There Innana dies, is reborn and returns greatly empowered by Her journey.

Traditionally, walking a Labyrinth echoes Innana's journey and it was likened to a pilgrimage to the Underworld (unconscious mind) and a return back to daily life. A journey to the deepest center of self and an eventual return with a better understanding of who we really are.

The Classic Labyrinth (right) is a rounded form with seven paths or rings. It occurs globally, from Cornwall and the Mediterranean, to Egypt, India and Hopi lands in North America. In Indian tradition, the seven ringed Labyrinth is said to mirror the natural form of the brain and eight-fold stages of the mind. It is also considered a protective symbol and useful as a visual meditation device during childbirth.

The Cretan Labyrinth, legendary home of the bull-headed Minotaur, is of the same classic form and it has been dated back to 3,500 BCE. It too is associated with journeying to the Underworld. The mythic journey through the Cretan Labyrinth is the hero's quest that follows Goddess Ariadne's thread to the central Goal.

Cretan Labyrinth making was seen as the carving out of the Divine, creating order from chaos. It's mythic creator was Daedalus the divine architect. The well known Minotaur story was probably originally an Underworld initiation involving the Bull God, a totemic being governing Earthly fertility. A psychological explanation of the Minotaur myth is described by Jill Purce thus:

"At the centre of the spiral Labyrinth, man meets and overcomes and thus unites with the Minotaur, the 'monster' of his own hidden nature, and is reborn to a new state of wholeness."

In America, Hopi Indian Labyrinths are explained as symbolic of Mother Earth and Father Sun. These Mandalas reveal the universal plan of the Creator. The cross in the middle represents the Father Sun and also the World Tree, axis of the universe. Hopi rituals of geomancy with the round Labyrinth involve priests making four furrows in the ground to harmonise the land with the Creator's plan, explained Evgeny Faydsh Ph. D (BSD EEG, December 2002).

Together with a global group of people, including other scientists, Faydsh had been going to the power places of the planet and building Labyrinths there. According to Faydsh, Labyrinths were once primarily centres for divination, used *"for obtaining information from the past and the future, and for connecting with other parts of the Earth."*

Throughout various eras, Labyrinths have been universally used as devices for ritual and celebration, where people have walked and danced, or where pilgrims in penance have followed the pathways on hands and knees. In Sweden, where the old ways have long persisted, Maypole dances are still sometimes held on the old Labyrinths.

Typically Labyrinths have three, five, seven, or eleven circuits that one follows, walking the pathways backwards and forwards before reaching the centre, a place of still meditation. The brain no doubt receives a stimulating balancing in the process of walking one direction and then the other, as in Cross-Crawling exercises.

Labyrinths have acted as portals, places of shamanic journeying for gaining information, power or healing. Spiritual initiation would have also been greatly facilitated within them. Faydsh describes Labyrinths as *"pyschotronic gadgets actively interacting with planetary energies and informational fields, and the psyche and energy of the person working with it."* They represent and act as *"embryos of order"*, some connecting everyday reality with the subtle worlds, he wrote.

Not all Labyrinths are big enough to walk in. Tiny Labyrinths etched onto flat stones, typically pieces of slate, were sacred objects that were once prized magical tools for British witches. The Labyrinth patterns were traced around with sensitive fingertips in order to enhance the mental state for magical working. Known as Troy Stones, they were used to contact the spirit world by inducing trance states, the fingers tracing around them while particular hypnotic tunes were hummed. Passed down from wise woman to wise woman, at the death of their last owner they were deliberately destroyed, thus few examples are surviving today. A rare example may be seen at the Witchcraft Museum at Boscastle in Cornwall.

In Scandinavia Labyrinths are numerous, especially in the isolated islands of Solovki, in the White Sea. At these ritual centres offerings were once made to the spirits of place and magical protection or healing was invoked. Many are found on shorelines, where they were walked around seven times by fishermen before they headed out to sea, as protection against violent winds and to shake off any attaching 'evil spirits' that might spoil their catch. One Labyrinth in southern Sweden had a reputation for curing mental illness and another was known to have been walked by a local shaman before he undertook healing or energy work.

Next page: An ancient Swedish turf Labyrinth.

Labyrinth Lore

A marker for pilgrims in Ireland, a fine Labyrinth carved on a stone, the largest in the British Isles, was found near the well worn pilgrim's path, St Kevin's Road, that links Hollywood with the monastic cente of Glendalough in County Wicklow, south of Dublin. The Hollywood Stone (below) now sits forlornly in the Dublin Museum.

The medieval Christian church adopted the Labyrinth for a time, using it to represent the idea of pilgrimage to God and a pathway to salvation. The Labyrinth at Chartres Cathedral is particularly famous. Like other medieval Christian labyrinths - it has eleven circuits.

These days many religious traditions have embraced the Labyrinth as a valuable spiritual tool. Whatever one's spiritual orientation, when walking a Labyrinth one can go into sacred space and become connected to divine energy. Effects can be energy enhancing and balancing for both the local landscape and individuals.

Labyrinths are now making a big comeback, with many being created in public spaces, while Labyrinth organisations are emerging in various countries, including an International Labyrinth Society.

Above: A public Labyrinth at Wesley Hill, near Castlemaine in central Victoria, features the different types of rocks found in the region.

In America, Alex Champion has been making Labyrinths since the 1990's at West Coast Dowsers' Society gatherings. He considers Labyrinths to be good focussing devices for Earth energy. Some people feel dizzy, tired, warm, tingly and other body sensations when walking the Labyrinth, he finds. Challenging feelings can be contemplated and spiritual healing facilitated. Effects of a walking meditation through the Labyrinth can be transformational and bring great inner peace, Champion enthuses.

Faydysh's group built their Labyrinths from whatever came to hand, be it stones, pine cones, small branches, or other vegetation. They found it was the proportions of the shape that was the more important thing. Most powerful effects came from labyrinths built in the most sacred of power places around the planet.

The group found that people who walked their Labyrinths while working on personal problems gained clear evaluation or new understandings of their problems. Also, as soon as the Labyrinths were constructed, the weather would immediately become sunny, even if it had been raining. Butterflies, birds, dogs and cows were very attracted to them, they also noticed. (Other writers say that rain has started to fall... Perhaps they all got what they were hoping for!)

Labyrinth Energies

Irish dowser Billy Gawn has written about an English Labyrinth in parkland, near Moulton in Northamptonshire, that the local council had constructed with gravel forming the pathways. *"I first observed this about two years ago, shortly after it was constructed, and there was a blind spring several yards away to one side. When I was there again, a year later, the blind spring was close to the centre of the Labyrinth,"* he wrote. *"I could continue to give many more examples where a structure and not human intent or activity had caused underground water to be diverted so that it is now underneath it."*

At the International Dowsers Congress in the UK in 2003 Shaun Ogbourne concurred. *"The Labyrinth pattern itself can draw in energy and water to around its location. But this happens more so with the actual regular use of that Labyrinth. The more energetic it gets, the nicer the atmosphere feels around a Labyrinth."*

Dowser scientist Jim Lyons also told the Congress how a Chartres Cathredral styled Labyrinth was made on an energetically neutral site. It has since attracted several underground streams of water to flow beneath it and there are also magnetic and gravitational anomalies now to be found there. These effects can occur whether the Labyrinth is made from basalt rocks or just sawdust, it has been found. Cats love the energy of Labyrinths too, he reported.

They are not alone in finding this water-attracting phenomena. *"Marty Cain, a dowser and labyrinth builder in New England, USA, has been finding this for several years now,"* said Billy Gawn. *"I am also hearing talk about this on the Internet. Labyrinths call in water? Apparently."*

Labyrinth Creation and Use

To make a Labyrinth of small stones, one needs a great many more stones than for a Stone Circle. Depending on the amount of space available, you need to work out the width of the pathways (a minimum of 300 mm/ 1 ft, if you want to walk it) and use that as a basic unit of measurement. Cut a stick, timber or cardboard piece so that it can be used for measuring and marking the lines. Make it a multiple of four times the path width and mark each of those units of measurement.

Labyrinth creation is begun with the laying of the cross in the centre, then the four 'seed' stones in a square are laid around it. The cross represents the Tree of Life, the World Tree.

From the entrance, known as the Mouth of the Labyrinth, the path goes left or right, depending on the orientation of it. Left turning paths are said to predominate in the northern hemisphere, so right hand ones may be more appropriate in the south. The centre is called the Goal.

The following diagram and photos show a simple method for easy labyrinth layout of the Classic Labyrinth, with the author's husband Peter Cowman and six students making the 6 m (6.5 yd) wide Vermiculite Labyrinth in around one hour. The width of its paths are that of the length of Peter's clip board, at 40 cm (1.3 ft).

Touchstones for Today

Labyrinth Creation and Use

Labyrinth Rituals

Outdoor rituals take us into altered states of consciousness, connecting us into other dimensions of place, as well as our own inner landscapes. We re-inforce sacred space each time we use our special stone arrangements as tools to access the Divine. Regular use keeps them well primed for the job.

Faydysh explains that the Labyrinth is *"not simply an architectural form but ...a psychotronic gadget actively interacting with planetary energies and information fields, and the psyche and energy of the person working with it."* It can act as a *"kind of mediator between the sacred world and the world of incarnate forms where we live,"* he said.

To inaugurate a new Labyrinth for the first time our own personally meaningful ritual of initiation can be devised and the space aligned to its most Divine purpose. For such a ceremony we might employ special mantras, incense, Reiki symbols or rune signs, musical instruments to play and the like. Creating a conducive atmosphere at night will involve soft, low lighting (no fluorescents!), such as candles. (Fire itself is invoked in Faydysh's rituals, when they use gunpowder and juniper for a lively inauguration!)

Visualisation is used to mentally connect a Labyrinth with the powers of Earth and cosmos. Faydysh recommends mentally placing a symbol of this connection - an image of the World Tree - at the central axis of the Goal. He says that the Labyrinth's centre represents the highest Divine principle and that it can be tuned to the highest powers of the universe, so that it *"starts to work as a receiver-retranslator radiating harmonious energies."*

There is an interesting parallel here with Australian Aboriginal ritual devices. Of a corroborree seen by a white observer in Steele's book, it was reported that in the Tucki Tucki Bora Ground centre was placed an upside down tree trunk, its roots spreading out like an umbrella above. This may well have been used for shamanic journeying, the centre of the Bora Ground being the typical location of an Earth Spiral, a subtle energy vortex power centre. This central power point provides a portal that can facilitate inter-dimension travel, while the tree symbolises the connection between Earth and Cosmos.

A Labyrinth initiation suggested by Faydysh involves entering the mouth of the Labyrinth slowly, holding some incense as you walk the path and chanting repetitive mantra (such as *Aum Mani Padmi Hum*) or prayers. Following the twisting path towards the central Goal, you focus on imaging all the negativity within you is dissolving into primary chaos.

Reaching the Goal, the incense may be placed there and one might focus on the *"endless axis of the World Tree"* that connects us to Heaven and Earth, he says. After such a consecration ceremony Faydysh noted of the Goal, that *"a powerful stream of sacred energy is formed above it."*

Upon leaving the Goal, one is symbolically reborn, so the focus is on one's re-creation, concentrating on abilities within the querent that are desired to be awakened or strengthened. Faydysh reported that, from practising this ritual: *"Almost all participants experienced creative breakthroughs... many discovered talents that were hidden. Others found new directions for their activity."*

The ritual may be done whenever balance or harmony is lacking in one's life; also when landscape energies need harmonising, he said, in which case one focusses on ecological goals.

A classic ritual walk in a Labyrinth is known as the Walk of Life. As you begin to walk, you review the stages of your life, with all its twists and turns. As you are coming out, you focus on the lessons learned. Normally one is somber or reflective on a Labyrinth walk. But it can be just as rewarding to be joyous and celebratory as well, as is appropriate for the occasion. Blowing bubbles as you walk, naming all the wonderful things in your life and practicing gratitude, are some of the many things suggested to do in a Labyrinth walk.

Touchstones for Today

The author's new Vermiculite Labyrinth was powerfully initiated by everyone walking it at once. The energies were really buzzing! Afterwards there was a wonderful time of peaceful silence, as participants reflected on the activity (see page 97).

More and more these days, Labyrinths are being used as psychological tools. As Dan Johnston, Ph.D, explains: *"A Labyrinth is an archetypal symbol for life's journey. An archetypal symbol is one embedded into mankind over a long evolutionary history.*

"The three phases of walking a Labyrinth [are, basically,] releasing, insight, and integration," he says, suggesting that Labyrinth walks are ideal for rituals of letting go, such as for for New Year's Eve, or for life's changing phases.

"A very simple walk," Johnston continues, *"is one of releasing, receiving and thanksgiving. The first half of the Labyrinth is walked with the intention of letting go of worries and fears. This is symbolized by walking with the hands palm down in a gesture of release. At the center of the Labyrinth the palms are turned up in a gesture of receiving whatever gifts of insight and peace are offered. Leaving the Labyrinth the palms are placed together in a gesture of prayer and thanksgiving as you walk towards the exit,"* said Johnston, of the Medical Center of Central Georgia, in a talk at the Labyrinth Society Conference of November, 2000.

A ritual to honor and nurture the Goddess within may also follow the threefold path. It begins with the release of negative energy, as you walk in, concentrating on letting go of worries and emptying your mind of stress. Or a particular Goddess might be invoked, reflecting on Her strengths or the lessons of Her myths. Then as you enter the Goal, you allow yourself to be receptive to insights and illuminations, preparing to receive the wisdom of the Goddess. Be open to receive Her gift. Then on the outward path assimilate new insights, think about integrating them into your daily life and manifesting positive energy. As you leave the Labyrinth's mouth, turn back to face the center, thanking the Goddess for Her gift. (A male deity might likewise be invoked.)

On a cautionary note, Faydysh recommends never to cross over the walls of a Labyrinth as *"this may destroy the energetic wholeness and all work will be for nothing."*

Chapter 6: Working with Stones

The author tunes in to the Touchstone at the Rock of Ages, near Maldon in central Victoria, Australia.

Touchstones

To contact and release the indwelling powers of sacred stones, the act of touching them, of making physical contact, is a pre-requisite. For example, several Irish monolithic Finger Stones of legendary hero Fionn Mac Cumhail (pronounced MacCool), have finger shaped indentations and they were believed to preserve the essence of the mighty hero's vigour. To gain these qualities oneself, it was a traditional practice to place one's fingers into the grooves on top of the stones. (Similar finger-like Pillar Stones are found in Germany and Brittany.)

A modern equivalent of this ancient idea, is that of *grounding* or *earthing*, where direct skin contact is made with the ground in order to release unwanted electro-magnetic charges, such as electro-statics, and also to absorb the life-enhancing energies of Mother Earth. On the simplest level, this is done by daily walking barefoot on bare ground, rock or wet grass. Many health cures have been achieved by this simple action, necessary because modern humans tend to insulate themselves from Earth's energies by the synthetic shoes worn these days. So the ancient idea of the Touchstone has special currency today.

A Touchstone allows us to connect with Earth spirit and deeply link to special places. It is the point where we can introduce ourself to a Sacred Site, when it's better not to go in too close or too fast, for fear of disturbing the place. Often the Touchstone of a site is a natural boulder that acts as an anchor stone for the devic guardians of place, who like to check out visitors and assess their intentions. Traditional ceremonies in the past would have, no doubt, taken place at the sacred Touchstones.

When the author has occasionally visited the Aboriginal Dreaming site called the Rock of Ages in Maldon, central Victoria, a pair of resident Serpent Spirits sometimes wrap themselves around the Touchstone (seen pages 113, 118 and the back cover). They do enjoy the appreciation of any sensitive observers, reported clairvoyant Billy Arnold.

A modern ceremony, based on Native American tradition, was filmed at the Rock of Ages Touchstone by the author (now in the film *Megalithomania*), who was visiting there with seers Junitta Vallak and Billy Arnold. Junitta placed offerings of sacred tobacco on top of the stone as she introduced us to the place, calling upon all the spirits of the land there to grant permission for our visit. With this respectful start we were able to go on to have a wonderful and insightful visit. When we left, a short ceremony was held at the Touchstone whereby thanks was given and we took our leave.

We may learn and enjoy much from traditional wisdom, but it is up to us to develop ways to communicate with the sacred Earth. Earth Ritual work can be simple. Saying hello, asking for permission to enter a site, asking for insights and giving thanks for all received, for example.

Daniel Johnston describes ritual as: "*Any action that speaks to the soul and the deep imagination, whether or not it has practical effects... Even the smallest of rites of everyday existence are important to the soul.*"

Touchstones epitomise the respectful return to nature that our society needs to make to become re-enriched and re-enchanted by the sacred land. We need Touchstones more than ever in today's world and we can easily install them in our own backyards.

Touchstone of Enchantment

Boulder,
Moist, mossified, fluoro-lime
and purple lichened
Seat of Wisdom
Solid portal
Carrying me
To the edge
Of Dreaming.
Enmeshing me
In enchantment of the land
I am Earthing,
Readily rebirthing.
Beholding the glory
and the Mystery.
Soul sustenance!
Being thankful
And returning,
Renewed, going out.
Touching stone
I am touched by this place
And it's true nature - otherworldly
In the resting place of Dragons
and Landscape Angels
I am grounded
With the souls of Kooris,
Past owners,
All around me.

Deviceless Dowsing

Attuning to the sacred we can use our whole being to merge with a site's powers and qualitites, using Body or Deviceless Dowsing. Our bodies have antenna-like structures, such as arms and hands, that we can develop to use as direct dowsing devices. We can train them to sense the inherent energies of a place or sacred stone and it is as much about how we focus on our intentions as it is about technique.

Our knees, feet and eyes also have keen sensing ability. It's a matter of simply asking them to be open to receiving certain energies and being aware of responses, such as the 'knee jerk reaction', or eye blinking. Dowsing comes naturally when we allow ourselves to try it out!

Many a time I have taught pendulum dowsing in conjunction with Deviceless Dowsing and there will be students who cannot get the pendulum to move much. Yet they will feel all sorts of sensations (tingling, warmth etc) in the palms of their hands when 'scanning' with them for energies. So they don't need a pendulum to 'read' a site!

Meditation with eyes closed can also be revealing. The mind is made a blank slate, open to visual or audial impressions that might be received. First impressions received are usually correct.

When our inherent sensing ability is activated, the power centres in the landscape can quickly become apparent. We can find the special places, where healing is facilitated and the veils to the other worlds are parted, and joyfully connect with their sacred energies. With psychic attunement to special sites, our spirits may be nurtured and our extra-sensory abilities developed and greatly polished.

Sometimes we may not know that a Sacred Site is in the vicinity, such as on a bushwalk in unfamiliar territory. But if our awareness is open, we may get a psychic prompting to stop and check. I call this the Check-In Point. From there, I go into meditation and ask if it's ok to go on. It may or may not be! Finding out first, is the polite approach.

Touchstones for Today

The author and husband Peter Cowman tune in to the Rock of Ages Touchstone.

Deviceless Dowsing

Dowsing students connect with Earth energies at the large group of Stone Circles near Odry, northern Poland.

Tools for Geomancy

Standing stones of all sizes are often used by today's dowsers and geomancers (Earth healers) as *"needles of stone"*, for their Earth Acupuncture ability to create energetic homeostasis, harmony in the landscape.

Lithopuncture is the term used by Slovenian author and geomancer Marko Pogacnik for his own geomantic stone work. Pogacnik is also a sculptor who carves special symbols onto his lithopunctural Pillar Stones, which are often commissioned by various European town authorities and inaugurated at official community events.

In Austria, a team of professional Druids working on eliminating 'black spots' on roads for the Austrian highways department use quartz Pillar Stones for Earth acupuncture, greatly reducing the road toll. And paramagnetic stone antennas, known as Towers of Power, perform Earth Acupuncture too, as the author has found from erecting several hundred around Australasia and beyond over the last 20 years.

As for Stone Circles - Dave Sanguine of the BSD Earth Energies Group notes that *"each stone of a Circle can have controlling effects on detrimental Earth energies"*. His colleague Billy Gawn also finds that Stone Circles can have far reaching beneficial effects on the local area. So when Gawn makes Stone Circles he seeks out a blind spring or water line crossing point and centres it there, as a means of controlling its energy. He suggested matching the size of the stones to the size of the energy being earthed. He also warns that *"the careless placement of objects in any energy field... can cause a reversal of the earthing of detrimental energy."* So Stone Circles need to be kept clear of clutter too!

Jim Lyons told the International Dowsing Congress of 2003 about a Stone Circle made by dowsers in Co. Roscommon, Ireland, in 2000. The 18 m (60 ft) diameter circle was located intuitively, the big rocks placed on 'messy' water line crossings, while the small rocks went on small 'perfect' crossings. It subsequently *"cleared the area of detrimental energy for some three miles around,"* he said.

Shaun Ogbourne continued - *"It was made with the intention of clearing the detrimental energies from as wide an area as possible. The bigger the stones the bigger the effects, so we used stones up to two tons in weight! (You can also use a larger number of more smaller stones.) Afterwards it was noted that the difference in the local community was dramatic. A lot of peoples' squabbling had quietened down."*

After making the Circle in record time, there was one more structure to be made, continues Tony Hathaway. *"This was the building of a Dolmen using three uprights and a large triangular slab of stone. The Dolmen was built over an ascending spiral of beneficial energy, using an angled capstone to reflect the energy back into a sphere within the chamber. It had the effect of acting like a transformer, which boosted the local supply of Earth energies. Everyone who sat within the Dolmen found it a very relaxing and peaceful experience,"* he said.

Although you can build a Stone Circle on energetically neutral ground, Ogbourne (who passed away in 2011) found that the best effects occur when an already energetic site is used and there is regular ceremonial use of the circle. Energy affects have been noted a mere three months after construction, he said.

Backyard megaliths can be enhanced with carved sacred symbols, some of which may have direct energetic effects. A simple petroglyph made on a rock can clear detrimental energies from a site or a home, Scottish researcher David Cowan has found. The act of chiselling a cup-and-ring

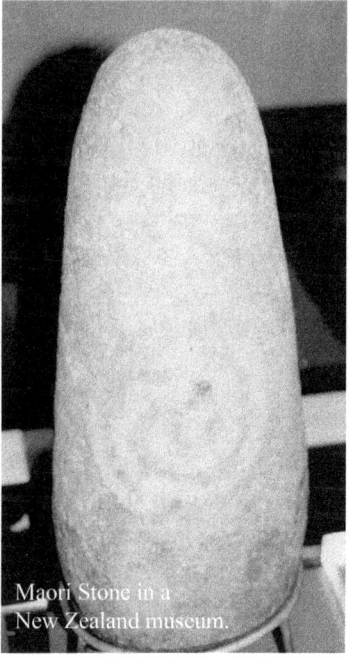
Maori Stone in a New Zealand museum.

or cup-and-groove shape into a rock sends out a protective circular energy field. When done in a certain way (written about in his book *Safe as Houses*), it has a clearing, harmonising effect, Cowan says.

Stone Circle Medicine

Jack Temple, a famous English dowser healer, has written about a whole new way of utilising the special energies of Stone Circles, in his book *The Healer*. Temple, who passed on in 2004 aged 87, was familiar with the idea that stones could convey healing energies. He often pulverised carefully selected stones in his clinic in Surrey and made tablets and tinctures from them.

One day he was invited to visit a Stone Circle with friends at Gors Fawr in the Welsh Prescelli Hills. There he discovered healing forces in particular stones that led him to believe that the site was once used like a *"Neolithic hospital"*. He could detect the powerful energy originating from the Circle some 900 m (1,000 yds) distant. At each stone he was able to dowse it's relative power by counting the rotations of his pendulum swinging over it.

Certain stones, he discovered, were able to capture and re-distribute energies from the Sun, Moon, Earth and planets. *"They release their own vibrational rays and also send that energy into the earth around them. Today I rely on a distillation made from grass clippings taken from the area around my own 'Neolithic Circle' for many of my important and effective treatments,"* he wrote.

Temple set up several such modern Circles of 16 m (52 ft) diameter, comprising 16 stones around a central cosmic energy absorbing stone. Each of the 16 stones represents a part or aspect of the body. Thus the area around each stone yields a remedy suited to that body part. *"We also have circles formed with a 4 ft (1.2 m) radius which are just as effective as a circle with a 52 ft radius,"* he wrote. A good way to absorb the energy, Temple found, was to get some patients to regularly spend time relaxing inside a medium sized Stone Circle, or sit on a chair under which a small Stone Circle has been placed.

For Temple, Stone Circle medicine became the most important aspect of his vibrational healing work. Following his passing, a couple of students rescued and re-erected two of the Stone Circles. There is now a Jack Temple Dowsing Academy and a Jack Temple Association of Healers, wrote Barry Witton in *Dowsing Today*, June 2007.

Unwanted Effects

British dowser Dave Sanguine warns of putting up a standing stone or stone arrangement that may attract unwanted energies. It could happen that underground streams may be attracted to pass beneath your home, if the circle is near enough to them. If shallow underground water flows are diverted from a nearby underground stream, or a blind spring appears, as has been observed, you might end up with geopathic stress (harmful energy) affecting the home as a result. Sacred space ideally shouldn't be the same as living space.

"I have inspected several places where Stone Circles were recently constructed and the builders did not take into account the underground water present on the site," Gawn has written. *"I found, at these, that under most of the stones small flows were present and that a blind spring or springs could also be dowsed within the area of the Circle."*

Not all Labyrinths turn out well for other reasons, too. I asked a friend how her Labyrinth was going. It had been made for both people and race horses to walk. I was surprised to hear that it didn't exist any more. *"We didn't like the energy of the person who had made it, nor the energy of the Labyrinth itself. So we had it removed,"* she explained.

Healing of Sites

Old megalithic sites might have been revered for their wonderful, healing energy for thousands of years, but these days, sadly, many have been energetically harmed by abuse and desecration. Some Sacred Sites have been scenes of massacre and genocide. The traumatised memory usually remains stuck in the atmosphere, especially in rock, and can still be palpable to sensitive souls even hundreds of years later. Fortunately it can be cleared.

On a more everyday level, people desecrate sacred sites in many ways, often without even thinking or knowing what they are doing. There are threats from litterbugs, mindless vandals, and, sometimes, from visitors who use sites for unwholesome magical ceremonies. Candle wax and even animal remains have been found at some sites (Rollright Stones, for instance). The atmosphere at a sacred place can become very unpleasant after such abuse.

Generally speaking, the energies of sacred space are easily tainted by peoples' inappropriate thoughts, feelings and actions. Conversely, we can cleanse, purify and energise them beneficially too, with our conscious and loving intentions.

Some sites and stone arrangements may need to have their energies cleared. One way to do this is for a group of people to enact a ceremony of healing intentions, involving the visualisation of colours (such as projecting white for purity, followed by green for balance and mauve for harmony), and the harmonious sounds of bells, bowls, gongs or digeridoo.

Singing, chanting (*Aum* is an excellent chant!) and dance too can be powerfully beneficial in helping to restore harmony to a place.

*Right: Dowsing students meditating at a megalithic site in Sweden.
Many Swedish stone circles are actually boat shaped.
This Stone Circle was in disarray until re-erected in the 1930s.*

Healing of Sites

Stone Circle Rituals

The power and magic of a newly made Stone Circle develops over time. Heightened energy will become apparent as soon as a Circle has been made and consecrated. But this will build to be much stronger after people have been interacting with it. Ed Prynn, an eccentric Cornish Circle builder written about by Rob Roy, has had hundreds of people visiting the Stone Circle in his backyard and they have delighted in touching and embracing the stones. *"Power came to my Stone Circle over a period of three years and it's now fully charged,"* he said. Ed and his friends like to dance and make music in the Circle. Running also gives mood enhancing effects. Running around inside the Circle five times *"makes you feel as high as anything,"* he enthuses.

When Ivan McBeth makes his Circles, he likes to align important stones to significant landscape features. He has written of aligning the largest stone at the north point of one Circle to the North Star. A little ceremony was conducted before the stone was put in place and beneath it were buried gifts of beautiful objects, herbs, stones and feathers. The south stone was next, with the same ritual process enacted.

Some stones were aligned to the sunset or sunrise positions of the equinoxes and solstices. Likewise at the Swan Circle, each stone had its own little ceremony, with gifts placed into each of the stone socket holes. Little stones and gifts from all over the world had been sent to him for this purpose.

After the Swan Circle was completed, just in time for the midsummer solstice and Glastonbury Festival of 1992, a torchlight pre-dawn procession by members of the Glastonbury Order of Druids brought them into the Circle for a ceremonial ritual of blessing the new sacred space.

But you don't have to be a Druid to do this! I believe that the rituals we create ourselves are the most powerful of them all! After your Circle is completed, an inaugural ritual of blessing can include these elements:

* A receptive mindset is needed. An initial period of meditiation may be useful.

* Visualise connecting the stones energetically together. This might be in the form of an image of a ring of energy encircling and tying them together. Chanting and toning all the while is good!

* If there is a central altar stone, connect that into the circle also, as well as to the Divine energies of above and below.

* Individual stones may become focal points for various energies. The four cardinal pointer stones, for instance, can act as portals to connect you with the energies of the four quarters/directions. So pay homage to the four directions at each of the cardinal points.

* Bless, dedicate and honour your Circle as a Sacred Site.

* Ritually walk around the Circle. In the northern hemisphere it is traditional to walk your Circle in a clockwise direction, so anti-clockwise walking in the southern hemisphere is a good idea.

* Visualise a dome of protection, an encompassing sphere of beautiful coloured light flowing around you and the Circle

* Finish your ritual with an offering of love and thanks, giving thanks to the stones, to the spirits of place, or deities and cosmos.

It is common for a nature spirit to want to move in and remain stationed within your Circle. This can be a great blessing, especially if you strike up a good relationship with it, by asking permission before you walk in, and sending it feelings of love and thanks at the end.

A little gift might go a long way too. A small piece of greenery or a flower, as is traditional in the Pacific region, or a little stone perhaps. By recognising and honouring the devas, you will greatly enhance the power and good feelings of a site.

Touchstones for Today

Above: With orbs all around, students tune in to the Stone Circles of Odry, northern Poland - one of Europe's largest groups of circles. A makeshift altar was on the ground, lower right: a pile of offerings, as below. Another Circle nearby is on the next page.

Joyful dance and music may be just as appropriate for your Circle ritual, as is solemn meditation. The sounds of Tibetan singing bowls, bells, gongs or didjeridoo, vocal harmonies and chanting will also accentuate energies and experiences. Circle space needs to be kept clean on all levels, and, with regular ritual use, the energy of the Circle will continue to grow and grow, to benefit ever wider areas.

A walking meditation in a Stone Circle can take you into the Dreamtime reality, if you are open and ready for it. It is a place for magical, deep connection with nature, a space for healing where one can be truly whole, in a temple of many dimensions.

If you are going to leave the area, your Stone Circle may need to be decommissioned. Before physically removing it, you might create a little ceremony of thanking it and saying goodbye, projecting the intention of de-activation. Make sure that any energy portals are requested to be shut down and sealed, as deemed appropriate (all of which is usually determined by dowsing).

Sacred Sites for Today

The Sacred Sites of old often acted as Earth's acupuncture points, allowing for the regulation of planetary homeostasis. Most of those ancient sites today are now in ruins or out of bounds for the ordinary person and thus inacessible. But we can re-create the sacred anew!

We can create centres for Earth ritual in the landscape and our backyards are a good place to start. Here, a sense of the sacred can be cultivated. We can go there in the humble state of bewonderment at the magic and power of nature; and honouring the web of life that sustains us all.

All forms of pollution should be avoided at our sacred places, especially the invisible kinds! Our thoughts and feelings are so powerful that we ideally never have cross words spoken there. The generation of harmonious energy should be paramount!

We need to make sure that no iron, or most other metals, are placed at our Sacred Sites either. Fairies and other devas traditionally detest them for good reason - metals do disrupt natural, subtle energy flows, such as geodetic (dragon) lines.

Likewise, no radio-frequency or other electro-magnetic pollution should interfere with a site. For instance, mobile phone towers or wireless internet. Electro-pollution is a serious problem in today's society and it easily overrides the good energies of sites. The author discovered the hill top Landscape Deva of an Aboriginal Sacred Site suffering in a high RF field, on her property in central

Victoria. The sensitive humans were reacting negatively as well! A few heart-felt messages to the neighbour were successful. They were able to turn down the settings on their cordless phone and wireless devices (some 100 m, 110 yd away) and the RF levels dropped to acceptable levels. The devas were very grateful too!

In other parts of the world (America and Sweden, for example), people create and place radiation reducing devices at the base of mobile phone towers and the like, to help nature and the devas cope with the high-tech world. (You can find out more on this subject in the author's film *Helping the Devas*, a short version of which is on YouTube.)

Tuning in to the sacred doesn't have to be done anywhere special, or in any particular manner, but when we create special spaces with stone arrangements, our own miniature Landscape Temples, these can develop fabulous energy and be extra-delightful to visit! To this end, Touchstones and the like can provide significant features of instrinsic power and with an enduring ability to delineate sacred space.

Billy Gawn and the Bronze Age Holestone (also known as Marriage Stone or Lovestone), near Doagh in Ireland's County Antrim. From the 18th century onwards young couples have exchanged marriage vows or pledged eternal love there, the girl placing her hand through the 8 cm (3 in) perforation in the 10 cm wide stone and clasping the hand of the boy. Some local people still do this, before or after their official wedding ceremony. Other Holed Stones had a reputation as portals where one looked through the hole, a window to other-worldly visions of the fairy realms.

References

Atkinson, Robert, *The Cult of the Circle Builders*, 1909, via *The Ley Hunter* magazine no.s 26 & 27, 1971.
Bednarik, Robert G, *Cupules – the Oldest Surviving Rock Art*, International Federation of Rock Art Organizations, Australia.
Bird, Christopher, *Divining*, MacDonald & Jane's, UK, 1979.
Bord, Janet & Colin, *The Secret Country*, Granada, 1976, UK.
BSD EEG (British Society of Dowsers Earth Energy Group) *Encyclopaedia of Terms suitable for those studying Earth Energies through Dowsing*, editor Billy Gawn, UK, 2000.
Cairns, Hugh and Bill Yudumduma Harney, *Dark Sparklers*, published by H Cairns, 2003, rev. 2004.
Comerford, Keiran, *Newgrange and the New Sciences*, CTM Books, Ireland, 2011.
Cook, Michael, *Dowsing Today* (BSD Journal), Vol 40 no 290, December 2005.
Cowan, David & Girdlestone, Rodney, *Safe as Houses?* Gateway Books, UK, 1996.
Cowan, David & Anne Silk, *Ancient Energies of the Earth*, Thorsons, UK, 1999.
Deveraux, Paul, *Places of Power*, Blandford, UK, 1990.
Deveraux, Paul, *Stone Age Soundtracks*, Vega UK, 2001.
Dorst, Henry, *Some Experiences of Dowsing among the Indigenous People of Canada*, British Society of Dowsers, Earth Energies Group newsletter, March 2001.
Evans - Wenz, W Y, *The Fairy Faith in Celtic Countries*, Citadel Press, USA, 1994 (original - 1911).
Flood, Josephine, *Rock Art of the Dreamtime*, Angus & Robertson, 1997.
Fox, Selene, *Circle* magazine, USA, December 2004.
Frances, Evelyn, *Avebury*, Wooden Books, Wales, 2000.
Gawn, Billy, *Black Chicken, White Egg*, British Society of Dowsers, Earth Energies Group newsletter (online), 2001.
Gawn, Billy, *Megalithic Structures: Why?*, self-published, UK, 2002.
Graves, Tom, *Dowsing*, Turnstone books, UK, 1976.

Graves, Tom, *Needles of Stone*, Turnstone, UK, 1978.
Graves, Tom, *Elements of Pendulum Dowsing,* Tetradian Books, UK, 2008.
Haigh, Mike, *New Insights into Rock Art*, from Northern Earth no. 65, adapted from *Making Sense of Prehistoric Art*, Richard Bradley, British Archaeology, Nov. 1995.
Harbison, Peter, *Pilgrimage in Ireland*, Barrie & Jenkins, London, 1991.
Hathway, Tony, *Building a New Stone Circle*, British Society of Dowsers, Earth Energies Group newsletter (online) 2002.
Hunt, Robert, *Cornish Fairies*, Tor Mark, Cornwall, (original - 1865), UK, 2004.
Ice Age star map discovered, BBC News Online, 9/8/2000.
Lisle, Harvey, *Stone Circles and Medicine Wheels*, American Society of Dowsers Journal, fall 1988.
Lisle, Harvey, *The Enlivened Rock Powders*, Acres USA, 1994.
Michell, John, *Secrets of the Stones*, Inner Traditions International, USA, 1989.
Moore, Alanna, *Divining Earth Spirit*, 2nd edition, Python Press, Australia, 2004.
Moore, Alanna, *Stone Age Farming*, Python Press, Australia, 2001.
Mullis, Diana, *West Country Fairies*, Bossiney Books, Cornwall, UK, 2005.
Norris, Ray P., Norris, Cilla, Hamacher, Duane W., Abrahams, Reg, *Wurdi Youang: an Australian Aboriginal stone arrangement with possible solar indications*, draft paper online, August 2011.
Ober, Clinton, *Earthing - the most important health discovery ever made?* Basic Health Publications, USA, 2010.
Pennick, Nigel, *Ancient Science of Geomancy*, Thames & Hudson, UK, 1979.
Pennick, Nigel, *Celtic Sacred Landscapes,* Thames & Hudson, UK '96.
Poyner, Michael, *Pi in the Sky - A Revelation of the Ancient Celtic Wisdom Tradition*, The Collins Press, Ireland, 1997.
Purce, Jill, *The Mystic Spiral - Journey of the Soul*, Thames & Hudson, 1974, UK.
Ring, Ken, *How to Make a Stone Circle – Southern Hemisphere*, Milton Press, Auckland, NZ, 2001. Website atwww.predictweather.com

References

Roy, Rob, *Stone Circles: A Modern Builder's Guide to the Megalithic Revival*, Chelsea Green, USA, 1999.

Screeton, Paul, *Quicksilver Heritage*, Abacus, UK, 1974.

Signature of Sky in Rock, in *The Hindu*, 19-04-06, via *Society of Leyhunters Newsletter*, May 2006.

Steele, J.G. *Aboriginal Pathways in southeast Queensland and the Richmond River*, University of Queensland Press, Australia, 1984.

Temple, Jack, *The Healer – the Extraordinary Story of Jack Temple*, Findhorn Press, UK, 1998.

Underwood, Guy, *Pattern of the Past*, Abacus, UK, 1972.

Versluis, Arthur, *The Elements of Native American Traditions*, Element, 1993.

Wakeman, William F., *Handbook of Irish Antiquities*, Bracken Books, London 1891, 1995.

Westbury, Virginia, *Labyrinths – Ancient Paths of Wisdom and Peace*, Lansdowne Press, UK, 2001.

Zuchelli, Christine, *Stones of Adoration*, Collins Press, Ireland, 2007.

Books on sensitive and sustainable living, esoteric agriculture and awareness of the spiritual dimensions of life and planet

Available at bookstores around the world
or buy direct from
Python Press - PO Box 929 Castlemaine
3450 Victoria Australia

www.pythonpress.com
pythonpress@gmail.com

Sensitive Permaculture
- cultivating the way of the sacred Earth
by Alanna Moore

This 2009 book explores the living energies of the land and how to sensitively connect with them. Positive and joyful, it draws on the indigenous wisdom of Australasia, Ireland and elsewhere, combining the insights of geomancy and geobiology with eco-smart permaculture design to offer an exciting new paradigm for sustainable living.

What has been said about this book:
"A delight to read" Callie *"You make permaculture so easy and alive---and sweet"* Joy, Taiwan *"Hard to put down"* Celia, Permaculture Association of Tasmania *"A very practical and thoughtful guide for the eco-spiritual gardener, bringing awareness to the invisible dimensions of our landscape"* Rainbow News, New Zealand
"An adventure in magical and practical Earth awareness" Nexus magazine

Divining Earth Spirit
- an exploration of global & Australasian Geomancy
by Alanna Moore, 2004

From English ley lines and fairy folk, to geopathic stress and the paradigms of the Aboriginal Dreamtime. This books explores the fact that the environment is alive and conscious!

"*A classic for anyone wanting to get involved with Earth healing. It contains information by the bucketload... The research that has gone into this book is incredible and no doubt will stir you into wanting to use it yourself"* Radionics Network, Vol. 2 No.6

"Love of the topic clearly shows, as Moore brings clarity and a sense of the necessity of personal involvement and engagement with the Earth. The great advantage of Moore's book is in its detailing all the salient aspects of Earth Spirit phenomena....all covered succinctly and with precision... the perfect introduction to the topic." Esoterica magazine, No. 4, 1995.

Stone Age Farming
- tapping nature's energies for your farm or garden

by Alanna Moore
2nd edition, 2012.

From Irish Round Towers to modern Towers of Power for enhancing plant growth. In this book ancient and modern ideas about the energies of rocks and landscapes are explored for practical use in the garden, including the application of dowsing, Earth wisdom and geomantic understandings. Eleven years after the 1st edition, Alanna has updated and revised this book, describing the outcomes of installing Power Towers in farms and gardens around Australasia.

What reviewers have said of the 1st edition (2001):

"Simply fabulous!" Maurice Finkel, Health and Healing.
"Quite fantastic." Roberta Britt, Canadian Quester Journal.
"Clear, lucid and practical" Tom Graves

The Wisdom of Water
by Alanna Moore, 2007

Water tends to vanish when human impacts are high. But we can reverse the trend and reconnect with the wisdom and healing powers of water.

Alanna Moore delves into water's mysterious origins and manifestations; its energetic and spiritual aspects; global traditions; as well as water in Australian landscapes. The potential of water divining, and 'new' water (created deep within the planet) provides hope for a sustainable, water-secure future, she believes.

What has been said of this book:

"Very invigorating. Highly recommended"
Jilli Roberts, Pagan Times, December 2007

"A great book!" Professor Stuart Hill

Python Press Books

Water Spirits of the World
- from nymphs to nixies, serpents to sirens

by Alanna Moore, 2012.

A follow-on from The Wisdom of Water, this book delves into even deeper esoteric aspects of water and the great variety of its spiritual denizens, including tales of real encounters with them.

What readers have said of the original (digital) edition of this book:

"A comprehensive collection of information and a rich insight into the world of water spirits ... including some wonderful stories of encounters with water spirits ... well researched and informative"
Martha Heeren, Dowsers Society of NSW newlsetter, April 2009.

"A wonderful resource book"
Morgana, Wiccan Rede, Lammas 2009

This *"joyful travelogue of water spirits around the world has been a journey inspired by love"* Anne Guest, Gatekeeper no. 26, UK

About the Author

Alanna Moore was a co-founder of the New South Wales Dowsing Society 1984. A professional dowser living in central Victoria, Australia, she is internationally known for her writing and teaching of dowsing and geomancy. She lectures worldwide and also makes films. A permaculture farmer as well, her writings are archived at geomantica.com as well as at Australia's National Library. Readers can subscribe for free to the Geomantica magazine.

www.geomantica.com

Geomantica Films
by Alanna Moore
Available on DVD from www.Geomantica.com
(See extracts of Geomantica Films on You Tube.)

* **The ART of DOWSING & GEOMANCY**
140 minutes of dowsing and geomancy training sessions with Alanna and her students.
Ideal for beginners.

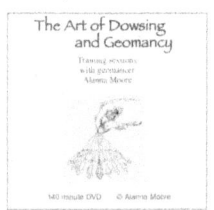

* **DOWSERS DOWNUNDER**
102 minutes of interviews and demonstrations with a diverse range of amazing dowsers filmed around Australia.

Three film series
(with each film around half an hour):

* **EARTH CARE, EARTH REPAIR**
(8 films)
Dowsing, Greening & Crystal Farming -including interview with broadscale wheat farmers about crystal farming. *Eco-Gardeners Down-Under* - featuring Bill Mollison and David Holmgren. *Grassroots Solutions to Soil Salinity* - with dowsers saving landscapes from dryland salinity. *Growing & Gauging Sustainability* - using Universal Knowledge to Brix meters. *Remineralising the Soil* - the value of paramagnetic rock dust and dowsing its qualities. *Making Power Towers* - shows the construction of a paramagnetic antenna, or Power Tower. *Agnihotra / Homa Farming* - an ancient Indian fire ritual that has marvellous effects on plant growth and animal and plant healing.

* GEOMANCY TODAY series
(5 films)

Megalithomania - Stone Circles and the like, from Europe to Australasia. *Divining Earth Harmony* - five geomancers talk about their diverse approaches. *Discovering the Devas* - yes, they are out here and you can dowse for them! *Helping the Devas* - an interview with Swedish dowsers who work with the devic kingdoms. *The Sacred World of Water* - from geo-mythology to a geomantic appreciation of water in the landscape.

* STATE of PILGRIMAGE series
(6 films)

Glastonbell Dreaming - interview with Australia's first white geomancer Phillip Simpfendorfer. *Pilgrimage to Central Australia* (exploring Aboriginal sites and culture). *A Thirst for Ireland* - indigenous Irish sacred sites and geo-mythos. Alanna Moore discovers her own Dreaming Land in County Limerick. *Bali: geomantic journeying in paradise* - from geomantic village and temple design to visiting a lake Goddess in the mountains. *South Australian Sojourn* - from Adelaide's Womandelaide festival to Hindmarsh Island and Kangaroo Island, discovering sacred sites and energies and indigenous geo-mythos.

Geomantica Correspondence Course

Diploma of Dowsing for Harmony

This correspondence Course imparts techniques and applications of pendulum dowsing that will help you to create a more energetically harmonious world and to potentially have a career doing this work. Originally written in 1989, many hundreds of students from around the world have enjoyed this opportunity for distant study. It has been revised and updated over the years. The Course can be bought in ten parts or all at once.

The Course includes comprehensive notes, dowsing charts and lists, practical exercises and personal Assessments from Course originator and internationally acclaimed tutor Alanna Moore, who has over 30 years dowsing and teaching of dowsing experience. You can start now or anytime and complete it in your own time, although generally it is usually undertaken over one or two years. No obligation when to finish. (It has also just recently been made available to a wider audience, for people who don't want to achieve a Diploma.)

The Ten Units of In-Depth Study:

Unit One: The Basics of Dowsing - Theories that help to explain dowsing. Clear, simple techniques and useful exercises.

Unit Two: Wholistic Diagnosis – The philosophical basis of holistic health and harmony, the importance of seeking balance of the mind, body, emotions, spirit and environment. Dowsing esoteric psychology with the Seven Rays.

Unit Three: Body Systems – An integrated approach to anatomy and physiology – from the physical to the energetic in global traditions, eg Chinese medical philosophy.

Unit Four: Analytic Dowsing – Dowsing for causative factors in disease, diet selection, food and water testing, allergen detection. The problem of pesticides, additives and pollutants in food and water and how to test for them.

Unit Five: Dowsing for Solutions – Selecting remedies and therapies by pendulum and Seven Ray analysis. Working with vibrational remedies made from flowers, gems, shells etc. Dowsing for homeopathic remedies.

Unit Six: Distant Dowsing and Healing – Remote health analysis and energy balancing techniques. Using symbolic patterns plus crystals and gems for remote healing work. Chakra balancing with the pendulum and more.

Unit Seven: Earth Energies and Health – How underground streams, geological faults and the like can cause geopathic stress. How to create and maintain harmony with geomancy and feng shui. Working with the devic dimensions – the nature spirits.

Unit Eight: Building Biology – Our homes are our third skin, and should protect us to some degree. Unhealthy homes can poison or irritate us with their toxic building materials and electro-magnetic fields etc. How to check for sick building syndrome and find healthier alternatives.

Unit Nine: Map Dowsing and Environmental Remedies – Distant dowsing by map to seek out harmful zones in the home and environment. Geomantic cures such as Earth acupuncture methods using copper pipes, crystals, etc to neutralise noxious zones.

Unit Ten: Towers of Power & The Professional Dowser - How to locate and make Towers of Power for land energising and harmonising. Professionalism in dowsing.

Some examples of comments received about the course over the years:

"I am thoroughly enjoying the course. ...Thanks a lot, the information has been of real practical help" Mrs R Ogden, Brunei Darussalam, Malaysia.
"I think it's an excellent course." H. Young, Mosman, NSW, Australia.
"Your section on chemicals is quite comprehensive.... I have found the course very informative." S. Becker, Perth, WA
"Another enjoyable unit and for me a great unfolding of my dowsing ability occurred. I think this was due to the amount of hands-on work in the lessons. It has built up my confidence..... The last unit of study has brought me to the finish of one and a half years of most enjoyable learning. I have reviewed my progress spiritually, physically and emotionally over this time and feel that personally I have grown in leaps and bounds. I feel that the connection with my true self/nature has been established." A. Rafferty, Lismore NSW.

The following comments were made about the original course textbook *The Dowsing and Healing Manual* by Alanna Moore (now part of the course):

"By far the best work on the subject I have come across."
Dr Jocelyn Townrow, Ph. D, BSc Hons, Sandfly, Tasmania.
"The best manual on the modern system of dowsing principles and information I have found...a splendid book." J Rubie, secretary New Zealand Dowsing Society, April 1990.
"A veritable bible for those interested in the background and techniques of dowsing." Jeni Edgely, Wellbeing magazine no 26, 1988.

See - www.geomantica.com/dowsing-correspondence-course